Find Joy, No Regrets

Cultivating Peace and Ease Through Choice

Lisa Marshall

Find Joy, No Regrets: Cultivating Peace and Ease Through Choice

ISBN: 9798297264229
Cover design by Jonathan Sweet
Cover photo by Dan Brehant Photography
Printed in the United States of America
First Edition

To My Father, Gene—

You lived to be 90, and every one of those years you spent as a quiet example for others to follow, and for me to emulate.

Kindness and compassion were your trademarks, peace and gratitude your steady guides. Like so many who knew you, I always felt special, loved, and truly seen in your presence. You were my biggest cheerleader, always curious about my life, always encouraging.

Every time we spoke, you'd ask the same question:

"Are you writing another book? I can't wait to read it."

Well, Dad—this one's for you. Thank you for being such an incredible teacher, a steady role model, and a never-ending source of inspiration.

Love,

Your "Baby Girl"

Acknowledgments

Writing this book was a deeply personal and often emotional journey, one I could not have made alone. It reflects not just my story, but the people, love, and support that helped carry me through the hardest chapters and into the most unexpected joy.

To Jonathan, thank you for loving me exactly as I am. For your honesty, your humor, your steady presence, and your deep compassion, especially for the parts of my heart that still ache. Thank you for never asking me to forget the past but instead helping me build a beautiful future. This book was shaped by your love as much as my own words.

To Peter, your memory is woven into every page. Thank you for the love we shared, the life we built, and the lessons that continue to guide me. Your story didn't end; it transformed. You live on in my heart and in the love, I now know how to give because of you.

To my children, Thomas, Sarah, and Zachary Brenner, and to my stepchildren, Sam and Sarah Marshall, and Zachary

Sweet, thank you for your patience, your grace, and your belief in me. Sharing life with each of you, watching you grow, love, and find your way, fills me with pride and awe. And to my sweet grandbabies, Sonny, Liam, and Harper, you remind me every day to keep choosing joy and relish in the wonder of what's to come.

To my close friends, who held space for me in the darkest days and celebrated with me in the brightest ones, thank you. You know who you are. Your presence reminded me that I was never alone.

To the Alzheimer's community, caregivers, advocates, patients, and families, thank you for showing me what resilience, love, and grace look like. You inspired my first book and continue to inspire my heart.

To the readers of *Oh Hello, Alzheimer's* who reached out, shared their stories, and asked me to keep writing—thank you for reminding me that sharing our truths matters.

To Robin, my spiritual sister and heart-centered writing coach, thank you for seeing this book so clearly even before I did, for holding me accountable with kindness, and for helping me bring my voice to the page with honesty and intention.

To my incredible book launch team; the generous early readers who gave their time, feedback, and encouragement. The friends who walked beside me with sharp eyes and open hearts. Thank you for your thoughtful edits, your honest critiques, and your well-timed encouragement. You helped shape this book with clarity and care, and you understood the deep vulnerability it took to share my story so openly. I'm grateful beyond words.

And finally, to the quiet guidance of something bigger than me, the whispers of intuition, grace, and divine timing that led me here, I offer my deepest thanks. You reminded me to trust the unfolding, to stay open, and to believe that healing, joy, and love are always possible.

Table of Contents

Foreword

When I think about the word *strength*, my mom's face is the first one that comes to mind. Watching her navigate life after losing Peter to Alzheimer's was one of the most difficult, yet deeply inspiring, things I've ever witnessed. But what truly stands out is how she channeled unimaginable heartbreak into something powerful—becoming an advocate for others walking a similar road, while never losing sight of grace, self-compassion, and the belief that life still holds joy.

This book is more than a recounting of her personal journey through loss—it's a roadmap for what comes next. It's about the quiet courage it takes to rebuild a life, not just survive one. In these pages, my mom opens her heart and shares what it looked like to reimagine her identity, rediscover her independence, and slowly—bravely—choose to love again. She writes candidly about the awkwardness and humor of dating after decades of marriage, the loneliness of starting over, and the often-overlooked beauty of dating *yourself* first.

Her story is one of resilience, yes, but also of reinvention. She reminds us that grief doesn't erase our worth or our capacity to love—it reshapes it. Her wisdom will meet you wherever you are: whether you're a caregiver, someone grieving, someone learning how to be alone, or someone hoping to be loved again. Through her vulnerability and honesty, she offers not just empathy, but a way forward.

For me, this book is a reflection of how my mom is not only one of the strongest people I know, but also one of the most generous. She's always been my best friend, and now, through these words, she's extending that warmth and friendship to anyone who needs it.

I'm endlessly proud of her—and so grateful she's chosen to share this part of her story with the world. I know it will resonate, uplift, and most of all, remind you that it's never too late to find joy.

Sarah Brehant, 2025

Introduction

"Do couple stuff," the photographer coaxed as Jonathan and I stood by the ocean.

The waves nudged us too, and the sunset beckoned us to stare at her. We stood awkwardly, putting our arms around each other's waists, and looked out to our right as the camera clicked. The water was calm, and the setting sun was a pure white light bursting against the water. Giggling, we tried to fulfill the photographer's request. It was all a bit cumbersome, doing couple stuff in front of my son-in-law, the photographer. Not sure what other couple stuff to do, Jonathan and I faced each other in an embrace. We kissed and giggled some more. My daughter Sarah stood off to the side, recording the sunset photoshoot.

The four of us had planned to eat dinner at the beachside restaurant, making reservations for when the sun would be setting. Dan wanted to capture Golden Hour and the magnificent natural lighting it provides. The Cayman Islands sun would not disappoint us. When we arrived, we ordered drinks, and I popped off to the ladies' room. Upon my return, everyone agreed the lighting was perfect and we should take advantage. Plucking off our shoes, we sauntered across the cooling sand to the photoshoot spot.

The temperature was perfect for a long beachy dress and sandals, and I remember feeling pretty. As we walked from the restaurant to the water's edge, I felt grateful. Grateful for

Jonathan, for my relationship with my daughter, for Dan and his passion for photography, and for the magnificence that surrounded me.

I was not privy to the conversation that had happened at our table while I was in the ladies' room. When I was out of sight, Jonathan reached into his pocket and said to Sarah and Dan, "I brought this." He popped open a tiny wooden box boasting a big, shiny engagement ring. Jaws dropped, and excitement mounted. When I returned from the ladies' room, the conversation leaned towards heading to the beach for photos. Sarah said, "Mom, you need lipstick," knowing I would want to look my best for what was about to be my engagement shoot! While we brightened our lips, Dan and Jonathan walked ahead of us to the perfect spot, where I joined Jonathan.

Funny, the gestures that come naturally when loving your partner seem to escape you when you are in the limelight in front of a camera. We fumbled a bit more, feeling awkwardly giddy.

Jonathan, trying to be creative in our couple stuff efforts, dropped to one knee and said, "What if I pretend to propose?"

I laughed and said, "Get up!"

Jonathan did not get up. He opened his hand to reveal that tiny wooden box and asked, "What if I actually proposed?" as he unveiled its contents. Stunned, I squealed, leaned over, placed my forehead on his, and grabbed his face, kissing his mouth. The tears started welling in my eyes, and joy mounted in my heart. After several moments, I stood up to look at the ring; a round 2-carat diamond in a four-prong platinum setting shining so brilliantly in the sun. It was perfect, exactly what I had always wanted. Dan's camera continued to click away, and Sarah held her hand steady, recording our beautiful moment.

"I guess I have to ask you to marry me. Will you marry me?" Jonathan asked.

"Yes, I'll marry you!" I cried, throwing my arms around his neck. An outburst of clapping and cheering came from onlookers at the restaurant. A moment to celebrate indeed.

Today, I sit in the office of my new home, which I share with Jonathan. We're excited to be planning our wedding. Today, my life feels surreal, and I reflect on how I arrived at the me I see in the mirror now. The processes, the work, the hope, and the trust in myself and *life* itself. The journey to get here is filled with necessary lessons, heartaches, and intense growth. I have found such extraordinary peace that I feel compelled to share my journey from devastation to joy.

CHAPTER ONE

A Glimmer of Hope

The devastation began 8 years ago in a primary care physician's office in 2017. "Peter's cognitive scores are alarming for a person with his education," the doctor had said. Our love affair started in 2001, and Peter and I were married in 2009 after an 8-year-long-distance courtship. We had been blissfully married only 6 years when the testing began to find out why Peter's cognitive clarity was fading.

Peter died in 2021, just 3 years and 8 months after receiving his early-onset Alzheimer's diagnosis. He was only 56 years old. We loved each other on purpose and cherished each other gently until the day he died. Watching someone you love so fiercely wither in mind and body is crushing. A part of me died, too, along with the dreams we had of our future together.

I had spent years caring for my husband's every need, and now, who would I care for? When my caregiving journey with Alzheimer's was over, I was left with an emptiness I could never have imagined. No amount of experience, knowledge, or research could have prepared me for what was coming. The

1

darkness, the loneliness, the fear, and the lack of purpose overwhelmed me.

What was my purpose now? There was nothing to look forward to. No eagerness, desire, or motivation. Without purpose, my soul felt dead and alone. I thought often of finding peace in my own death. It seemed no one could understand my devastation. Loneliness smothered me even while I was surrounded by a roomful of people, wearing my magic marker smile. How could I go on, I wondered.

The feeling of hopelessness was too much to bear. I remember writing "I want to be a beacon of hope. I want to live my life in such a way that others are not afraid to dream" in my book, *Oh, Hello Alzheimer's*. What I did not realize was that I had to become a beacon of hope for myself. Mustering up an unthinkable amount of courage and bravery to create a new life, filling the voids that trauma and grief so generously gave me.

Grief is the kind of potent you snarl at and quickly pull back from, like a horrible odor or a grotesque sight. Grief is persistent and demands attention, and you must give her the attention she wants, allowing her to visit. But don't allow her to stay. Grief can quickly transform you into an unrecognizable version of yourself. The day drinking started. I would pour a glass of wine to stave off the panic of being alone and numb the sharp edges of truth. Peter was gone, and my life was changed forever. Our five children, all in their 20s and 30s, had lost their father and stepfather. I had lost my husband, my friend, and my lover. I could not find peace in spending time alone with myself. There was no color, only gray.

I counted the hours, watching the clock until I could go back to bed. Bed seemed to be the only comfort I could find. The mattress held my heavy body. The blankets hid my truth.

Friends and family would ask how I was doing, and I habitually lied, saying I was fine. I had neither the strength nor trust that anyone could even comprehend what I was feeling. As I shrank further and further into hopelessness, I did not want to go on living without Peter.

The nights, specifically the darkness, were horrific. Chewing on Xanax just so I could lie in the shadows without panicking became the norm. Many nights, anxiety smothered me. I could not breathe, and I would jump from the bed frantically fumbling for a light, running out of the room into the lit hallway for safety. Running, trying to escape the anxiety.

You cannot run from anxiety and panic, but I discovered tools to ward off these responses ever so gradually. Sleeping with the lights on helped. All the lights, not just a night light. When the intense fear came, I could open my eyes in the light, and the fear would subside. Eventually, I was able to turn off one lamp and then another until I was sleeping with just a night light. I asked myself to be very brave and stay with my feelings of fear for just a second or two, before jumping out of bed. Feel the fear and sit with it for just one or two seconds to see what happens.

I faced fear head-on to see if I felt worse or perhaps better by choosing to fight rather than flee. I felt inspired to explore what was scaring me. Why was I so frightened? I was frightened of being alone. Why did I feel safer in the light? I felt more in control, being able to see that everything was peaceful. The more I confronted the fear, the less cowardly I became. Facing those spine-chilling feelings just one single second at a time encouraged me to sit with the fear longer until eventually it dissipated. I had conquered the darkest depths of my suffering. There it was, a glimmer of hope, and my spirits began to lift.

Lisa Marshall

CHAPTER TWO

Teaching What We First Need to Learn

There's a quiet, almost sacred irony in the lessons we're called to teach. So often, they're the very things we once struggled to understand, to embody, to believe. That's not a weakness—it's a map. Life has a way of guiding us through the fire so we can one day offer warmth to someone else.

For me, the lessons I've lived weren't handed to me—they were unearthed, often painfully, through caregiving, grief, being bullied and abused, healing, rediscovering myself, and choosing peace over chaos, again and again. Each of the themes in this book—intentionality, radical acceptance, self-talk, forgiveness, boundaries, community, and blooming into your full self—wasn't simply something I learned and then shared. These were lifelines I reached for. Tools I sharpened by necessity. Truths I grew into. And now, truths I get to share.

I don't arrive in these pages as a guru or guide, but as a fellow traveler with a lantern. The light I offer you is the light I had to kindle in my own dark seasons. It's the same light that helped me find my way through heartbreak, caregiving, and the long, uneven path to healing. And now, it shines not just to illuminate my own next step, but to serve as a quiet beacon for others walking their own uncertain roads.

I didn't set out to become a teacher of these things. I was simply trying to survive them. But over time, I began to see a pattern, not just in my story, but in so many others too. The very places where we've struggled, fallen short, or felt lost often become the places where we carry the most wisdom. Our wounds become portals to empathy. Our questions turn into guidance. And slowly, the lessons we once desperately needed begin to live in us so fully, they can't help but flow outward. That's the quiet miracle of it all: we don't need to have everything figured out to be of service, we just need to show up with honesty, heart, and the courage to share what we've lived.

That's the gift of authenticity. When we allow ourselves to be fully seen, even in our tender places, we become proof that healing is possible. Hope is contagious. And the more we live in our truth, the more we light the way for others to do the same.

Before I could share any of the lessons my life has taught me, I had to face the shadows I'd carried for years, stories I'd never spoken aloud, wounds I'd hidden beneath layers of silence.

There were moments of cruelty, bullying that left me questioning my worth, and an abusive relationship that tried to steal my voice. For a long time, I carried those things quietly, assuming they said something about who I was or what I deserved. But I've learned — the things that happen *to* us don't get the final say—unless we let them. Our healing begins the moment we decide our story will not end in the shadows.

There are the parts of my story I held back, the quiet battles fought in secret. But now, I'm ready to bring them into the light—not to relive the pain, but to show how those dark places shaped the woman I've become. And most importantly, I choose to let those experiences be the fuel that lifts me, not the chains that hold me back.

I've carried these stories quietly for decades, and I'm finally ready to release the weight of the emotions I've held for so long. Sometimes I wonder why I've spoken so openly about Peter and our journey with Alzheimer's, yet kept these other experiences tucked away. The truth is, these particular memories were wrapped in shame. But over time, I've come to understand *why* I felt that way—and that understanding has allowed me to meet myself with compassion instead of blame.

As a pre-teen, my body developed earlier than most, and my breasts grew faster and larger than my peers'. That made me stand out—and not always in a good way. The boys were curious, and the girls saw me as a threat. Kids at that age can be incredibly cruel. In junior high, I was bullied mercilessly. A rumor spread that I was stuffing my bra with tissues, and soon, tissues would mysteriously appear on my desk or tucked into my clothes as I walked down crowded hallways. The rumor caught fire quickly, and I felt completely helpless. Boys would openly ask me if it was true, and people would call my home repeatedly, saying painful things like "slut," "whore," or "you stuff [your bra]" before hanging up. Looking back, I can only imagine their cruelty came from jealousy. Still, at the time, I was overwhelmed with shame and embarrassment, often walking the school halls with my head low, trying to disappear beneath the weight of humiliation.

During that summer, after eighth grade, I had the opportunity to go to the local pool for the day with a family friend. It was a lovely summer treat and I was looking very forward to the day. I hadn't thought about the cruelty I had

7

endured during the school year and was enjoying the freedom of summer break and the joy of friendship.

The large, shallow pool was packed with kids, and I decided to go to the deep pool, which appeared to be quieter. My friend was enjoying the warmth of the sun on her beach towel. Slipping into the water, I allowed my body to sink. I enjoyed the peacefulness of the underwater world. Everything was so still and quiet. Shapes were fuzzy and voices muted. Although it was less crowded, there were still quite a few people frolicking there, including some of the teenagers who had bullied me during the school year. We were 13 that summer. I was wearing an orange flowered bikini.

Three boys spotted me. These were not just any three boys; they were jocks. These popular, now-freshman boys were tall, with arms and legs everywhere. I was not in their friend group, no, of course not. They were strong and loud and confident. I was none of those things. They could get away with anything. I had witnessed it: teachers looking the other way, excusing their boisterous behavior.

The lifeguard blew the whistle and announced, "Adult Swim." The deep pool started to slowly empty as swimmers headed toward the ladder. The three boys swam toward me and surrounded me like sharks. I was trapped in the corner of the pool, where I couldn't stand.

"Aren't the tissues in your bathing suit getting wet? Let's check if she really stuffs," said the ringleader. He grabbed at my bikini top, and I fought fiercely to keep my breasts covered, but I felt the cold water on my skin. I was exposed. Their huge groping hands made me feel small and helpless.

One boy opted out at that point and left the pool. I thought the remaining two boys would follow suit, but they did not.

They fought harder, untying the string around my neck and yanking at the fabric until I was completely exposed.

I remember the ring leader's big red face near mine, his wet hair dripping on my face, and their huge hands all over my breasts. The water was deep, and I kept going under the water, coming back up, gasping for air. It was unbelievable that this was happening. It was unbelievable that this was happening in broad daylight in a crowded swimming pool.

We were now the only three people left in the pool. The boys' Stretch Armstrong limbs quickly propelled them to the ladder and out of the pool. I could hear the boys laughing as their wet feet hit the cement, leaving me terrified in the corner. I was the sole person in the pool. My wet bikini top was floating in front of me, and I was gasping for air, my arms crossed, hiding my breasts. I felt small, violated, and humiliated.

Adults began getting in the pool as I fumbled, trying to put my top back on, and quietly slithered out of the pool. I quickly walked to the blanket we had spread out, and I covered my body with a towel for the remainder of the pool day. I never spoke of the incident.

After that traumatic event, my self-worth plummeted. I felt unworthy and undeserving to be a part of the popular friend groups and sought to find a connection with kids like me. I found it in a group of friends who were popular—popular for getting in trouble. My new rebellious friends introduced me to risky and exciting behaviors like skipping school, smoking in the bathroom, smoking pot, and drinking. They introduced me to older boys.

At sixteen, I found myself drawn to a nineteen-year-old boy. We were reckless together, tangled up in youth and impulsivity, and I became pregnant. The relationship felt like a whirlwind of emotion and escape—until it didn't. Not long after we moved in together, his words turned cruel. The verbal abuse crept in quietly at first, then quickly escalated. The physical abuse followed. And because of everything I'd experienced before—the bullying, the shame, the deep-rooted feeling that I wasn't enough, I believed, in some quiet, distorted way, that maybe I had done something to deserve it. That somehow, this was the love I had earned.

I dropped out of school at sixteen, leaving behind the familiar comforts of home and friends as we moved to a military base in Quantico, Virginia, where he was stationed with the Marine Corps. I was far from everything I knew, and the loneliness settled in quickly. As the days wore on, that loneliness gave way to fear—fear that took root the more I witnessed his short temper.

We rented a run-down, one-bedroom apartment, and I tried my best to make it feel like home. But there was nothing homey about it. Roaches scattered inside the kitchen cupboards. Neighbors screamed through the walls. Traffic blared outside. I missed my family. I missed my life. We fought constantly—about everything and about nothing. He was loud, commanding, full of swagger. He sneered, barked orders, and belittled me until I shrank.

Pregnant and scared, I ached for my parents—for someone to wrap me up and tell me it was going to be okay.

In my fifth month of pregnancy, I went alone to my scheduled ultrasound. The room was still, filled with quiet hope. Then silence. The doctor couldn't find a heartbeat. I remember the words, but more than that, I remember the feeling—as if the ground beneath me cracked open. I was confused, terrified, and heartbreakingly young. Just sixteen.

On December 21st, 1982, the doctor removed the fetus. Four days later, surrounded by family, I sat through Christmas, hollowed out and grieving.

My parents and siblings urged me to leave him. They offered their homes, their hearts, and their help. I tried. I left— three times. And I went back—twice.

It took a year and nine months, and the birth of my oldest son, for something in me to shift. I realized that protecting myself wasn't enough anymore. I had to protect *him*, too. That clarity gave me the courage to do what I hadn't yet done: to be vulnerable. To speak up. To ask for help—and accept it. I had to advocate for both of us. And I had to get the hell out. Leaving wasn't easy. But staying would've cost us both far more.

Once the baby and I were settled back at my parents' home, I made an appointment with the high school principal. He greeted me with compassion and grace; I had missed an entire year. Thankfully, I had earned enough credits to pick up where I left off—and walk across that stage with my class.

When I look back on those painful experiences of bullying and abuse, I understand why I felt so deeply ashamed and embarrassed. Being bullied shattered the fragile sense of safety and trust I had in the world. The rumors alone were brutal, but it was the invasions of my body and space that left deeper wounds—the girls slipping tissues into my clothes to mock me, the boys trying to rip off my bathing suit top to see if I was "stuffing." Those weren't just cruel pranks. They were violations. And later, when I found myself in an abusive relationship—enduring not just demeaning words, but physical harm—I recognized a devastating pattern: my boundaries were continually crossed, and I had begun to believe I somehow deserved it. At that age, the need to belong is primal. When you're judged, ridiculed, or harmed by your peers, or by someone who claims to love you, it becomes dangerously easy to question your worth, to shrink yourself to survive. But even in that shrinking, a quiet voice remained, insisting I was not that person.

The hardest part is how cruelty can get under your skin, making you believe the lies others tell. Even when you know deep down they're untrue, the weight of those words and actions can make you feel invisible, isolated, and powerless. But here's what I've come to believe—and what I want you to know too: none of that shame ever belonged to me. The shame was never mine to carry. It was born from others' cruelty, not from who I am. The fault and responsibility lie entirely with those who violated my boundaries. My body and my story are worthy of respect and kindness.

Each of those experiences—each cut, each sting—tried to tell me who I wasn't. But after the noise faded, I started to hear a quieter, kinder voice inside me. The one that said, "You are still whole. You are still worthy. You still have a right to be heard." That voice became my lifeline—the lesson I needed to learn, so I could one day teach it. We often find ourselves teaching the very lessons we most need to learn.

Choosing to listen to that inner voice, day after day, wasn't always easy. But it's what brought me here—and it can bring you here too. I learned that no one can humiliate me unless I give them the power to do so. If you're carrying shame, pain, or doubt, know this: you're not alone. You are so much more than the story others have tried to write for you. Your voice matters. Your story matters. And you deserve to bloom exactly as you are.

Questions to ponder:

1. What is one life lesson you've had to learn the hard way—and how has it shaped who you are today?

2. Have there been times in your life when you felt silenced, small, or ashamed? What helped you begin to reclaim your voice?

3. Is there a part of your past you've been afraid to share, and what might change if you gave it air and compassion instead of secrecy and shame?

Lisa Marshall

CHAPTER THREE

Practicing Intentionality

My first grandson arrived the year after Peter was diagnosed. Nothing made me happier than spending time getting to know Sonny and spending every Sunday together while his parents worked. Peter, Sonny, and I spent the entire day playing, dancing, laughing, and learning together as we pushed the must-dos into the not-so-important column. We focused on the preciousness of right now, and I realize now how relevant that focus was.

The month after Sonny turned two, I made the difficult decision to pause our Sunday playdates. I could not keep both Peter and Sonny safe as they each required a great deal of supervision. There were jealous spats over toys and my attention, and I was spread too thin. They were both so important to me that I could not risk one of them getting hurt. Peter died the month after I made that decision.

Sundays came and went, and I missed playing with Sonny but had difficulty finding the strength to be happy and playful. Resuming the playdates now would mean leaving my comfort zone of despair. I'd be getting up early, showering and dressing, which had become a rarity as I hadn't been motivated to give a care. But this 2-year-old gave me purpose and something to look forward to. I made the call to my son asking him if we could resume our playdates, even though it would take a great deal of vitality I wasn't currently feeling.

The first time Sonny came into my house after Peter died, he announced, "Poppy all gone". He already knew and seemed to exude an air of peacefulness about it. Energy is contagious, and I somehow started to feel more peaceful, too. Once we resumed our playdates, Sonny and I shared memories of Poppy, and our bond grew deeper. Sonny and I spent more time with Peter in his last two years of life than anyone else did. I realized that Sonny had become my support and my community, and we shared a sacred connection. I felt as though Sonny was the one person who truly understood my loss, and I'm convinced this 2-year-old saved my life.

I eagerly anticipated our time together and looked forward to something for the first time since Peter's death. Clutching his little body close to my heart, silently allowing the tears to flow, pent-up grief was replaced by a sense of support. A mutual joy emerged as we both cherished our playdate memories with Peter. We shared memories that no one else in the world knew about and that made me feel less alone.

My hopelessness lifted a little more after each playdate, and I came to the realization that there were indeed things to look forward to. When I began intentionally focusing on the good feelings I experienced, they seemed to multiply. I had a choice: dwell on sorrow and what was lost, or embrace the joy and experiences still possible in my life.

It didn't take long to realize that this was something I wanted to practice: intentionally focusing on feeling good. I wasn't just recalling memories of our playdates to lift my spirits; I discovered that sharing these experiences with others brought me even more joy. The happier I became, the more peaceful I felt, and hope seemed to ignite within me. That sense of hope and lightheartedness became utterly addictive.

Like anything, cultivating intentional happiness took practice. It required me to focus on what brought me joy and remain present in that feeling for as long as possible while consciously choosing not to dwell on my loss. Pulling myself out of my gloomy comfort zone demanded extraordinary attention and energy. I wasn't always successful. In the beginning, I often found solace in my grief, wrapping myself in its familiar weight. Sadness had been my constant companion throughout my journey with Alzheimer's, making it easy to sink back into. But deep down, I wanted to feel good again, and that desire felt instinctively right. The very fact that I was yearning for something brighter was a good sign of healing. With that in mind, I made a commitment to myself not just to find joy in fleeting moments, but to make it a way of life again.

When I made this commitment, I discovered two important things almost immediately. One, I could not be gloomy and grateful at the same time. Two, practicing gratitude was not only easier than intentionally being joyful, but it made my joyful practice easier! Those two emotions seemed to go hand in hand, and I was addicted to both.

At first, this realization caught me off guard. I had spent so much time navigating the weight of grief, responsibility, and uncertainty that I hadn't considered how gratitude might shift my emotional state. But gratitude seemed to unlock something within me. When I found even the smallest things to be grateful for—my morning coffee, the kindness of a friend, the warmth of the sun on my skin—it was as if a window opened, letting in fresh air after being in a stuffy room for too long.

I started noticing the moments when gloominess crept in. It wasn't that I ignored sadness or pushed away difficult emotions, but rather, I saw that when I actively acknowledged something I was grateful for, it was impossible to hold onto that heaviness in the same way. Gratitude didn't erase the hard things, but it softened them. It reminded me that even in grief, even in exhaustion, something good still existed in my life.

The connection between gratitude and joy became undeniable. I hadn't yet built a structured habit around gratitude—I wasn't keeping a journal or setting aside time for it—but the awareness alone began to shift my perspective. Gratitude wasn't just something to practice; it was something to lean on. And the more I leaned in, the easier joy became.

This realization felt powerful. If gratitude could create space for joy, then maybe I had more influence over my emotional landscape than I had ever realized. Maybe joy wasn't something I had to chase down or manufacture—it was something I could invite in, simply by acknowledging what was already good.

Questions to ponder:

1. When you are in despair, can you force yourself to envision a joyful memory or thought until it becomes a joyful feeling?

2. When you've mastered intentionally feeling joyful, can you practice pushing out feelings of despair as they arise, replacing them with more positive thoughts?

3. Who or what provides that sacred space and feeling of gratitude to lift you up when you are down?

CHAPTER FOUR

Radical Acceptance

I first heard the words "radical acceptance" from the private nurse I hired to help care for my husband, Peter, in the last months of his life. The nurse had expressed concern to Peter's hospice nurse about my abrupt attitude change. When she relayed their conversation, she noted that I "didn't seem upset anymore." She worried about my mental state yet, in reality, I was more at peace than I had been in months. A peacefulness had come over me, and I felt as though I was helping Peter to die, rather than trying to keep him alive. The nurse continued by saying that Peter's hospice nurse was a Buddhist and had explained that I was practicing radical acceptance.

After some research, I learned that radical acceptance is closely related to Buddhist teachings. The concept is simply accepting reality without resistance or judgment or wishing things were different, even when circumstances are painful. Acceptance doesn't mean you like the situation, but that you stop resisting it. Acceptance didn't mean I wasn't grieving; I simply accepted Peter's ensuing death.

The term "radical acceptance" was popularized by Tara Brach, a psychologist and meditation teacher, who merges Western psychology and Buddhist practices. She reminds us to be present, giving our full attention to the immediate moment. This practice encourages us to actively recognize and accept emotions, circumstances, and thoughts without trying to change them.

For most, this exercise requires thought and intention to achieve active participation and a lot of practice to become intuitive. Some may find themselves tumbling back into the dark comfort of "Why is this happening to me?" and other feelings, causing emotional struggle. That's perfectly normal. In my case, I did not find myself intently working to accept my reality; radical acceptance melted over me.

My husband was in a hospital bed in our living room. He was no longer thrashing around, agitated, and full of fear. Although he was still confused, he was peaceful, and so was I. I did not make a conscious decision to start practicing this foreign concept; in fact, I had never heard of it. But something profound happened to me, like a switch. My mind had reframed the situation for me, from "Why is this happening to me?" to "How can I be more present?" and "What can I learn?" and "How can I help ease Peter's transition?"

My mind was no longer frantic and overwhelmed with thought. When we are consumed by what we could've done or what we should do, we cannot be completely in the present moment. We are second-guessing decisions made in the past or worrying about what the future will bring. I found myself intentionally immersing myself in the moment to experience everything that life was offering then and there. My uncluttered mind offered me a beautiful glimpse into a peaceful and quiet serenity. I loved that feeling, and I wanted to spend more time there. I craved it.

Letting go of the suffering caused by notions like "Why is this happening to me?" resulted in a sense of freedom. Releasing control of the situation slowed my mind and extinguished any fictitious to-do list to change things. I was now focusing on the way things were instead of the way things should have been. This newfound concept freed my emotions to be more loving and attentive, living more fully and mindfully. The things that soothed Peter in his last weeks of life also soothed me. The lights were dim, lavender was diffused in the room, soft music was playing, and the room was warm. We held hands, and I stroked his head. I gently cared for his cracked lips, squeezing water from a tiny sponge onto them, coating them with moisturizing lip balm and kisses. We seemed to be journeying to death together without resistance.

I had wholeheartedly embraced this new peaceful state of acceptance while caring for Peter, but after he died, I struggled to practice radical acceptance at all. A new level of devastation had arrived, and it was more comfortable for me to immerse myself in loss and grief. "How could this happen to me, to us?" I cried. "Who am I now?" "What am I supposed to do without him?" The new reality of Peter's death was too heavy for me to accept, and the peaceful concept I had learned once again seemed foreign.

Recognizing when I was resisting reality was the first step in recultivating radical acceptance. Emotional discomforts like anxiety, hopelessness, self-doubt, and frustration signaled struggle. Physical cues like fist clenching and muscle tension, especially in my jaw or shoulders, indicated resistance. Thoughts such as "Things were supposed to be different," and "What am I going to do now?" were signs I was trying to control the situation. I needed to let go and find that cozy, peaceful space I loved so much.

Slowly, as I started to heal, I learned how to acknowledge the pain without fighting it. I learned to sit with my emotions, even if only for a few seconds, and recognize and accept that grief is a natural part of love and loss. I concluded that grief and joy could co-exist and, to this day, they still do. Allowing myself to experience both loss and joy simply meant making space for sorrow *and* new happiness.

Through research and practice, I learned practical action steps to implement after recognizing resistance. Mindfulness is the first step for me. Clearing out the clutter in my mind. Mindfulness for me is not only being present without thinking about the past or the future, but exploring the moment. While having a meal, how does each bite taste? Can you explore the different flavors and aromas? Are there different textures? What are the ingredients? How does it feel in my belly? When having a conversation with a friend, I love exploring their energy and facial expressions while they're speaking. It's my goal to hear and absorb their words rather than use the time to think of my response. How does the tone of their voice change? How am I feeling about the conversation? Feeling gratitude for everything in the moment is a gift.

To explore mindfulness, I began meditating again, a tool I had tried using many times but had given up on. I had previously subscribed to the popular notion that "I can't quiet my mind." What changed my thinking was giving myself grace. Meditation is gentle and forgiving, with no right or wrong way to practice. When practicing a ten-minute guided gratitude meditation, the guide said, "If your thoughts wander, that's ok. Everyone's thoughts wander. Just come right back to my voice." Well, that reframed meditation and gave me grace and permission to meditate my way, even if my thoughts wandered. Closing my eyes, resting, and listening to a guided meditation has become a daily ritual in my quest for peace and ease. In my experience, great ideas often pop into my head when I sit still enough to clear my thoughts!

Reframing is a powerful tool I utilize whenever I hear words coming out of my mouth that are not in alignment with my optimistic attitude. Shifting from "Why did this happen to me?" to "What can I do now?" changes the way you think about a situation, enabling you to shift your mindset from struggle and frustration to empowerment and acceptance. Reframing offers benefits like reduced emotional suffering, increased emotional resilience, and a greater sense of control.

Mantras and affirmations are encouraging and keep your thoughts framed positively. A mantra is a word, phrase, or sound you can repeat to anchor your thoughts and beliefs, often used in meditation. Mantras help to keep my thoughts from wandering. Often, I use my breath to guide the mantra. As an example, I might inhale and think "I feel peaceful," then exhale and think "Life is easy," repeating to keep my mind anchored. Affirmations are phrases that encourage a positive mindset or belief. The goal is to reprogram your subconscious mind by consistently repeating new beliefs and perspectives. Some examples of positive affirmations could be, "I accept my situation exactly as it is." Or "I choose to be peaceful and happy," or "I relinquish control and embrace life as it comes." Repeating an affirmation that is unique to your situation is a terrific reminder of how you want to think and feel.

Perhaps you may not fully believe in your mantra at first. If you have the desire to believe it and transform negative thoughts into positive ones, keep repeating your mantras and affirmations. You get to choose what to think! I've always loved this saying: Your thoughts become your beliefs, your beliefs become your words, your words become your actions, your actions become your habits, and your habits become your character.

As I became more skilled, radical acceptance became intuitive and a way of life. However, the path to proficiency is often paved with common barriers.

- Guilt: Feeling as though moving forward means forgetting. Find ways to honor your loved one that make you feel good. I find sharing stories or laughing about memories with people who knew Peter to be extremely helpful.

- Regret: Wishing things had gone differently. This is out of our control and a wasted moment in the present time. If you're thinking about the past, you cannot be in the present moment.

- Fear: Feeling uncertain about the future. If you're worrying about the future, you are not living mindfully in the present moment. You're missing life!

- Social Stigmas: Pressure from others about what your grief should look like. It's none of your business what other people think.

Beyond grief, radical acceptance can be a transformative practice in many areas of life, especially when we cannot control the challenges we're faced with. Empowering yourself to utilize this concept in relationships, careers, parenting, physical health, and mental well-being will become a powerful tool.

Questions to ponder:

1. Can you recognize when you're resisting and let go of things out of your control?

2. How does reframing negative thoughts feel to you?

3. What areas of your life can benefit from practicing radical acceptance?

CHAPTER FIVE

Connection to Community

My mother would tell you I came out of her womb, insisting, "I can do it myself!" and it took me over five decades to realize that I most certainly cannot. Life, I mean. I cannot do life by myself. And why would I want to? I have discovered friendships, found solace, embraced the concept of community, and given friends the gift of my vulnerability.

The first five decades of my life were filled with the belief that Wonder Woman status was only achieved by doing everything independently. A team of one. The reward I sought was validation from others that I had done a fantastic job. My competitive nature yearned to be number one at everything, and I wanted all the credit for doing it alone.

Caring for a loved one who needs 24-hour care is mentally, physically, and emotionally exhausting. I had reached a crossroads-I could care for Peter on my own or ask for help so Peter could have the quality of care I wanted him to have. It was difficult for me to understand that asking for help was not a sign of failure but a sign of strength. I was forced to ask for help because, of course, I wanted Peter to be well cared for. In doing so, I realized the many benefits of community, not just during my journey with grief, but every day.

"People want to help, they just don't know what you need." My friend Lori Riley told me. I'll never forget that. When Lori changed my perspective to what the helper felt, I had an "aha" moment. I asked myself, "How do I feel when someone asks me for help?" I feel needed and valued. I'm eager to assist, and it makes me feel happy. A sense of community is born, a fulfilling bond that makes me feel as though I'm making a difference. Surely if I felt this way about helping others, they must feel the same about helping me. By asking for help, we allow someone to thrive and feel a sense of purpose.

Embracing my new perspective, I developed the concept of the FOUR A's OF SELF-CARE to help me enlist support in a way I could accept emotionally during my caregiving days. While I introduced this essential caregiver concept in my first book, *Oh, Hello Alzheimer's*, its value is universal, offering guidance and support in any situation.

1. ACCEPT: Accept help when someone offers something, anything. This will encourage them to ask again and get you in the practice of saying yes more often. This could be something as simple as someone offering help during meal prep at a dinner party you're hosting. "Can I help you with anything?" A previous version of myself may have said, "No, I'm good, I got it," based on my ingrained theory of 'I can do it myself'. But a new, improved version will gladly say, "Sure! Can you fill the glasses on the table with water?" or "Would you mind cutting the bread and putting it in this basket?" People want to help, they just don't know what you need. By

saying yes, my to-do list is reduced, and I can be more present instead of distracted by tasks. The helper feels a sense of inclusion and belonging, and we both have more time to catch up and relax.

2. ASK: Ask for help before you need it, being proactive rather than reactive after you've unraveled from feeling overwhelmed. In the case of caregiving, when we wait too long, our thoughts become insurmountable, and we begin to feel alone and sad. Before burnout begins, enlist someone to help. In everyday situations, if you see an opportunity for someone to help, invite them! We ask young children to help all the time to teach them to be helpful, but asking for help from peers is sometimes difficult. I'll use another dinner party example. I host family dinners for my children and grandchildren once per month. Each family brings something to contribute to the dinner, whether an appetizer, dessert, or a side dish. I firmly believe that many hands make light work. I sometimes ask the kids for dinner requests beforehand, and my son, Zachary, who is an Executive Chef, requested "sautéed broccoli with lemon zest and Parmigiano." Everyone had arrived, and they gathered in the kitchen. Conversations were boisterous while everyone began catching up and nibbling on appetizers. I was managing the timing of the salmon, potatoes, and the 'sautéed broccoli with lemon zest and Parmigiano', trying to read the instructions with one ear to all the

conversations. I started to feel a bit overwhelmed and pulled from the conversations I wanted to be a part of. I invited my son to help with the broccoli. "I'm not sure what your expectations are with the broccoli, would you mind showing me?" He was happy to help, and a teaching moment ensued. By asking for help, my task list was reduced, I didn't need to be preoccupied reading a recipe, and I could be more present in conversations in the room. Zachary felt a sense of purpose and pride, teaching his Mom something new, and I learned a new way to cook broccoli by blanching and roasting it.

3. ARTICULATE: Articulate precisely what you need. As a caregiver, I may have had a personal doctor's appointment and could not take Peter along. Or perhaps I needed a nap to recharge? Maybe a small errand like going to the post office that I just couldn't get to? This relates to caring for children as well! In a more generic sense, as partners in a relationship, we need to maintain balance in the household tasks. Perhaps one partner is overwhelmed with work, kids, volunteering, or life in general! Articulating what you need to your partner can regulate the balance. "I know it's my turn to make dinner, but I need to tackle some things that I've been neglecting. Would you mind making dinner tonight?" People want to help, they just don't know what we need. Without this articulation, your partner would not know you're feeling

overwhelmed. Your stress could turn into misplaced impatience towards your partner. While you're making dinner, thoughts of your to-do list prevent you from being present. By enlisting your partner's help, they feel valued, you tackle the few neglected tasks, and sit down to dinner feeling grateful and connected, able to be present in the conversation.

4. ACTUALLY: Even after developing this theory of good intentions, as a stubborn independent caregiver, it was hard for me to kick-start, so I needed to somehow hold myself accountable. When someone asked me, "Please let me know if you need anything," I made a demand on myself. Instead of offering the usual empty promise, "Ok, I will," I promised myself I would say, "ACTUALLY." That one word caught my friends' attention, and they perked up, eager to hear how they could be of assistance. By saying, "Actually," it held me accountable to ask for something I needed. The first few times were cumbersome, and I soon realized I needed to have a mental checklist of some things I could always use help with. As a caregiver, the list is long: "Actually, can you drop this package off at the post office for me?" or "Actually, I have a doctor appointment I need to go to next month, could you stay with Peter?" or "Would you mind pulling my trash cans out to the street? I can't leave Peter alone, and it's too difficult to do it with him." Generally speaking, going back to the dinner party example, "Can I help you with

anything?" If I'm struggling mentally to accept help, I can say, "Actually, can you slice the bread and put it in this basket?" In the example of asking your partner to make dinner, they may notice your high-stress level and ask, "You seem overwhelmed, can I help with anything?" By responding with "Actually," you're holding yourself accountable to accept the help and release the guilt. The more often you ask for help, accept help, and articulate what you need, the easier it gets. By practicing this theory, you're creating a community of support.

By radically accepting that I needed support, I began to recognize more and more benefits. Letting go of the burden of my self-imposed guilt was freeing. I discarded the fear that asking for support was burdensome and embraced the feeling of belonging and connection. Letting go of my need for complete independence allowed my vulnerability to ease. My independence evolved into interdependence—a beautiful balance between self-sufficiency and relying on others, a balance between giving and receiving. I found a middle ground that felt both empowering and comfortable.

What is our responsibility as community members? Again, the balance of giving and receiving must be harmonized so the scales of support are even. Each community member should feel seen and heard, and as though things are fair. If parents are doing all the household chores while teenagers play video games in their rooms, it's perfectly acceptable to ask, "What have you done today to contribute to our community?" In being fair to fellow community members, we should also hold ourselves accountable, examining if we are contributing fairly to the community.

Questions to ponder:

1. Can you release the social stigma that equates asking for help with failure, and begin building a community of support?

2. Can you reframe asking for help as not a burden, but an opportunity for someone to give and support you?

3. Are you contributing fairly to the communities that support you?

CHAPTER SIX

Connection to Self

Self-support isn't a luxury; it's a necessity. I've learned that caring for myself is the foundation for everything else in my life, and I've made it non-negotiable. Though I've been retired for years, my days are anything but slow. I pour my energy into being a volunteer, gramma, author, speaker, mother, friend, and fiancée. Each of these roles requires my time and heart, but I've come to understand that I can't fully show up for others unless I first show up for myself.

Often, people feel guilty about taking time for themselves, and they may see self-care as selfish. I felt this way, too. Slowly, I learned that nurturing myself is the most important thing I can do for myself and my relationships. Creating space for self-nourishing reduces my anxiety and promotes restoration. The better I feel, the more fully I can show up in my relationships.

What is self-care anyway? For me, it's many things, as I've become an expert! First and foremost, it's giving yourself permission to feel good without guilt. Self-care is giving yourself grace and recognizing when you need rest, healing, and recovery. It's loving yourself enough to provide balance instead of burnout. Self-care is self-love. A simple question to ask yourself is, "What makes me feel good?" A walk in nature, yes, please! A hot cup of tea or 30 minutes with a book? How about a nice bath or 10 minutes of meditation? I find petting a kitty on my lap while watching TV is very soothing! A phone conversation with a loved one, a hard workout, or a glass of wine. Self-care is a quiet cuddle with someone you love, looking at old photographs, or sleeping late. Self-care is a massage, a facial, or a pedicure. Self-care is caring for yourself the way you care for others. The way you would care for your child, your partner, or your best friend. Self-care is loving yourself. When we intentionally care for ourselves, we encourage resilience and self-confidence.

Self-care is easier when we surround ourselves with people who prioritize it. The late Jim Rohn, known as the father of personal development, said, "You are the average of the five people you spend the most time with." If we spend time with people who prioritize wellness, emotional support, optimism, and personal growth, we are likely to do the same. Evaluate your circle of five: "Are the people I spend the most time with encouraging and supporting me or draining my energy and bringing me down?" The energy, habits, and attitudes of those in your inner circle influence your energy, habits, and attitude. Ask yourself, "Who lifts me up? Who holds me accountable? Who makes me feel inspired?" Support is most impactful when it comes from the right people. Spending time with negative or stagnant people can drain your energy and motivation. A support group that sits in a circle and spends time together commiserating is not beneficial to your growth and well-being. Intentionally choosing those in your support network is essential to how they will influence you.

Community is an excellent form of self-care, as self-care does not always mean solitude. Belonging is an essential part of self-nourishment. The right community or communities can offer different support. For instance, I find the richest community to be my family. When my children and grandchildren are in our home for dinner, I am surrounded by family traditions and memories. We strengthen our bond, hold each other accountable, problem-solve, and catch up on everyone's current events. The world seems to disappear, and it's simple to be present in our conversations because I'm so interested in what they have to say.

Volunteering for the Alzheimer's Association is another community for me. The staff and fellow volunteers have become friends, and we share a common bond. The bond of arduous caregiving and ambiguous grief. We are all working towards the same mission, to end Alzheimer's, which instantly forms a robust connection. Individually, we are small, but as a community, we are a powerful force, each playing a vital role in a greater mission.

A community can be a friend group or a single person; a group you go camping with, try new restaurants with, or play board games with. It's not what you do necessarily, but the connection you feel when being with them. Are you supported? Do you have things in common to talk about? Does the overall attitude energize your well-being? Do you support each other? I have girlfriends whom I can chat with on the phone for hours. We can cry together or belly laugh so hard that we can't breathe. Those special friends who make me feel seen and heard. Friends with whom I share a sacred bond through silly experiences or traumatic heartache. We show up unconditionally in these relationships, sharing bonds that are balanced and mutually beneficial to our well-being. That's community and healthy reciprocity.

The balance of giving and receiving is one that must be tended to often. I intentionally take inventory of my schedule frequently and adjust as needed. If I find myself feeling overwhelmed, I know it's time to take a look at my schedule. Maybe I've volunteered for too many events or activities. If so, I examine whether these events are long-term or short-term. If they're mostly short-term, my schedule may let up in the coming weeks, offering me a light at the end of my tunnel. Do I have self-care scheduled in the near future, like a lunch with a friend, or a pedicure? Focusing more on self-care and cutting back on obligations resets me back to balanced harmony. I feel at peace most often when my giving and receiving are in harmony.

Questions to ponder:

1. What are your self-care practices? Do you make them mandatory?

2. Who are the five people you spend the most time with? Are adjustments needed, either spending more time with people who influence you positively or less time with people who drain your energy?

3. Are you evaluating your balance between giving and receiving to maintain harmony?

CHAPTER SEVEN

Choosing Your Battles

There's a peaceful, quiet wisdom that comes with intentionally choosing your battles. One of the most powerful lessons I've learned through caregiving, grief, healing, and simply living is this: you don't have to attend every argument you're invited to. You don't have to react to everything. You certainly don't have to say yes to every demand on your time and energy. Choosing your battles isn't about giving up. It's about choosing *you,* your peace, your priorities, your presence.

It's easy to think of the phrase "choose your battles" only in terms of conflict. And yes, sometimes it's about deciding whether or not to speak up in a conversation that's going sideways. But more often, choosing your battles shows up in the small, quiet moments. It's about asking yourself: *Where am I using my energy? Is this really worth it?*

Sometimes it's not about standing your ground with someone else, it's about noticing how you're spending your day. Am I vacuuming right now because it actually matters… or because I feel like I *should?* Could I leave the dishes in the sink for twenty more minutes and take a walk or call a friend instead? Choosing your battles might be as simple as choosing *you*, choosing rest, movement, joy, or quiet over the pressure to always be productive. I've had to be intentional about this. By practicing, I find it easier to let go of that sense of obligation to complete things that truly don't matter.

Some battles are absolutely worth choosing. The ones that involve your values. Your truth. Your voice. When someone tries to dismiss your experience or cross a boundary you've set, that's a moment to stand tall. I've learned the difference between holding my peace and betraying myself, and they are not the same thing. It takes practice to recognize that tension in your chest or your gut that says, *This matters. I need to speak up.* It takes just as much wisdom to feel the peace that comes from letting go of something that truly doesn't deserve your energy. That quiet wisdom is empowering.

Caregiving taught me this in the deepest way. With Peter, especially toward the end, I learned that not every truth needed defending. Correcting him when he was confused or when he believed something that wasn't real didn't help either of us. But joining him in his reality, even if it didn't make sense to me, brought comfort. That preserved Peter's dignity and my peace. That *loved him well.* In those moments, I learned that peace was more important than being right.

As his disease progressed, it became clearer and clearer that our remaining time was limited. I let go of things like house cleaning, lawn mowing, and sheet changing. Those things meant nothing, but took up precious time. I spent more time sitting on the front porch with Peter, cherishing our remaining time, and asked for help with the rest. The chores would be there later, but Peter would not.

Sometimes, the biggest battles are the ones we're fighting with ourselves. The old stories. The guilt. The pressure. The "I should have..." or "I didn't..." Those internal battles can be so heavy. Sometimes we just have to ask: *Is this helping me heal? Or is it keeping me stuck?* Some battles need facing. Others need releasing. And that's okay.

I've come to believe that choosing your battles is really about deliberately choosing your *life*. We only have so much energy, so much attention, so much heartspace. We get to decide what's worthy of it. Not everything needs a reaction. Not everything needs a front row seat in your mind, and not every demand needs a yes.

Take inventory. Notice where your energy is going. Protect your peace like the precious thing it is. Let yourself off the hook when you need to, and don't be afraid to stand up when something truly matters. Choosing your battles doesn't make you passive; it makes you powerful. It means you know yourself well enough to walk away when it's time… and to lean in when it counts. There's a quiet strength in discernment. In knowing what's yours to carry and what's not. In realizing that you don't have to respond to everything, prove anything, or explain yourself to everyone. You can simply choose peace, and that choice, that *self-knowing*, is powerful.

There's a kind of inner confidence that comes from walking away from something that doesn't deserve your energy. From saying, "This doesn't align with who I am or how I want to feel," and letting it go without guilt or explanation. That's not weakness. That's wisdom. That's self-trust.

When something *does* matter, when it touches your values, your boundaries, your loved ones, your truth, you'll feel that too. It's the moment you realize *this is worth standing up for. This is a battle I will not walk past.* Maybe it's speaking up for yourself, or maybe it's advocating for someone you love. It could be saying no, or yes, or not now. Choosing your battles means you can meet those moments from a place of calm strength, not reactivity.

It's not about avoiding hard things. It's about aligning with the *right* things, the things that reflect who you are and what truly matters to you. It takes courage. It takes clarity. And it takes practice.

In my own life, especially in the seasons of caregiving and grief, I learned that my energy was sacred. I couldn't waste it trying to be superwoman, justifying decisions, or pleasing every person. I had to be intentional. I had to listen to myself. Over time, I realized that choosing my battles wasn't about controlling the world around me; it was about honoring the world within me.

That's the power. That's the peace. That's the freedom that comes when you trust yourself enough to know when to lean in, and when to lovingly let go. And here's something I've come to deeply believe: when you start choosing your battles with intention, the people around you notice. Whether you realize it or not, you become an example of calm, of groundedness, of clarity. You show others what's possible when someone lives from a place of peace rather than constant reactivity. You give permission, without saying a word.

In a world that often rewards overdoing, overthinking, overreacting, and overexplaining, it can feel radical to pause and choose a different way. But that quiet kind of strength? It's contagious. When someone sees you calmly walk away from a conversation or situation that no longer serves, or kindly decline an obligation that doesn't align, or step back from a power struggle without needing to win, it makes them wonder if they could do that too. If maybe they don't have to exhaust themselves in every direction. If maybe they can stop hustling for worth and instead start honoring their peace.

We teach people how to live by the way we live. When we model this kind of discernment, not with pride or drama, but with grace, it creates a ripple. It lets others know they're allowed to choose peace, too. That boundaries aren't selfish. That walking away from chaos isn't quitting, it's wisdom. That quiet doesn't mean weak. That knowing when not to fight is just as powerful as knowing when to speak up.

Sometimes, especially with the people we love, modeling this is more effective than anything we could ever say. Our kids, our friends, our coworkers, they may not change overnight. But they'll remember how it felt to be around someone who didn't live in constant tension. Someone who let go when it was time, and leaned in when it counted. Someone who was brave enough to protect their peace.

Choosing your battles isn't just a gift to yourself- it's a quiet act of leadership. Of love. Of legacy. It shows those around you what it looks like to live with intention, and more importantly, it teaches them how to treat you. To protect your energy without apology. To listen for what truly matters and let go of the noise. You model what it means to choose peace over perfection, presence over pressure. That's how change begins. Not always with loud declarations, but with steady choices. Daily decisions. And the quiet courage to live aligned with what matters most.

Questions to ponder:

1. What battles are you currently fighting that may not be worth your time, energy, and peace?

2. Are there battles you've been avoiding that may be worth leaning into with love and clarity?

3. Who in your life might be quietly watching how you handle conflict, stress, or decision-making? What are you showing them?

CHAPTER EIGHT

The Voice That Lifts Me:
The Foundation of Self-Talk

In the years I spent as a caregiver, I became intimately familiar with the weight of self-doubt. Was I doing enough? Was I making the right choices? I second-guessed myself constantly, even when I was running on empty. After my husband passed away, that doubt didn't disappear—it just changed form. Instead of questioning my caregiving, I started questioning who I was without that role. The silence left in grief was loud, and I found myself filling it with harsh self-judgment.

But here's what I've learned: The voice that speaks to us the most is our own. And if we're not intentional about the words we use, that voice can become our biggest critic instead of our greatest source of strength.

I see this in the *Oh Hello Alzheimer's* community all the time—caregivers doubting themselves, grieving spouses wondering if they should be "further along," people feeling lost in the transition from what was to what is. But if we're willing

47

to rewrite the script in our heads, we can begin to change not just how we see ourselves but how we experience life.

Confidence doesn't come from having all the answers. It comes from trusting ourselves enough to take the next step, even when we don't know exactly where the path leads. It's about replacing guilt with grace, fear with resilience, and hesitation with belief in our own ability to navigate whatever comes next.

The words we say to ourselves matter. And just like I had to learn to change my own inner dialogue, I want to invite you to take a closer look at yours. What would happen if you spoke to yourself with the same kindness you offer to others? If you gave yourself permission to believe in your own strength? If you let go of the "shoulds" and embrace where you are, exactly as you are?

Let's explore how shifting our self-talk can change the way we move through caregiving, grief, and every stage of life beyond it. Because the voice that matters most is the one inside you, and it's time to make sure it's speaking with love.

Growing up, I was the youngest of six children. My personality then was a combination of testing boundaries and shrinking into myself. I liked the thrill of pushing limits and trying new things, but I was painfully insecure. The thought of speaking in front of a classroom of my peers or walking into a room of adults I didn't know made me so nervous that my palms would sweat, and I would become nauseous. It wasn't because I was shy; it was because I had little self-confidence.

My insecurity stemmed from limiting beliefs that filled my mind. The deep-seated belief that I wasn't good enough, combined with an overwhelming fear of looking foolish, held me captive. It silenced my voice, stifled my actions, and kept me from stepping into opportunities that I longed for. Every time I considered taking a leap, self-doubt whispered that I would fail, that I wasn't capable, that I didn't belong. I wanted to try out for cheerleading; I would've been awesome, but that fear became a cage—one I didn't even realize I was locked inside of.

Then my mother offered me some wise advice that I carry with me to this day, "Walk in there like you own the joint!" She just announced it as though it could be so! Her version of fake it til you make it, I suppose. I kept her in my ear during oral book reports, when I was afraid to talk to the popular girls in school, or when I was called on in class. Even as an adult, her words instill confidence.

I worked in radio, selling advertising, which I loved. I had just been promoted to sales manager and was tasked with leading weekly sales meetings. I was terrified. That insecure little girl was always there poking at my self-confidence. "You have no idea what you're doing." "You're going to look like a fool." "Some of these people have been here much longer than you, what makes you qualified?" the voice in my head rattled. A classic case of imposter syndrome. In my mind my boss had made a mistake, hired the wrong person. I wasn't qualified for this! But my mother whispered in my ear. And again, I walked in like I owned the joint week after week. I made the choice to listen to her voice until I believed it myself.

We speak to ourselves constantly, more than anyone else. The silent words we use internally become the scripts for how we navigate our lives. Our scripts become our beliefs and dictate how we see ourselves, how we show up in the world, and what we believe we are capable of. If our inner dialogue is filled with doubt and criticism, we move through life hesitantly, second-guessing our every step and not trying out for the cheerleading team.

But if we speak to ourselves with kindness, encouragement, and trust, we build the confidence to take risks, embrace opportunities, and grow. Our thoughts shape our reality—what we tell ourselves daily becomes the foundation upon which we build our lives. I used my mother's voice as a surrogate for my own until I gained confidence and freedom from limiting beliefs.

Both negative and positive self-talk are powerful. Empowering yourself to be your own inner cheerleader will inspire confidence and self-growth. Confidence isn't just about achievements, but about the way we speak to ourselves. The more we affirm ourselves with phrases like "I am capable," "I am learning and growing," and "I trust myself," the more resilient we become. Practicing negative self-talk like "I'm not good enough," "I'm not qualified," or "I'll probably fail" increases anxiety, self-doubt, and reliance on others for validation and reassurance.

Investing in your thoughts requires intentionality. That little girl still shows up sometimes before a big speech, but changing my limiting thoughts from, "I'm not going to be able to deliver this speech effectively," or "I'm not qualified to be talking to this group of professionals," to "I'm the expert, this group is here to hear what I have to say," or "I'm going to change their perspective or inspire growth today," ensures those negative thoughts don't become beliefs.

Thoughts become beliefs through repetition, emotional reinforcement, and validations from experiences and external influences. The more we think about something, positive or negative, the more we believe it. Our brains are wired to seek patterns and consistency. Our minds are always listening, absorbing, and reinforcing the stories we tell ourselves. The more we repeat a thought—whether it lifts us up or holds us back—the more deeply it takes root.

Questions to ponder:

1. What's the biggest limiting belief you want to change?

2. What positive, uplifting phrases can you start using to shift this belief?

3. How can you become more aware of your inner dialogue and listen to what you're saying to yourself?

CHAPTER NINE

Shaping Belief with Self-Talk

Neuroscientist Dr. Jeffrey M. Schwartz explains, *'The brain is a creature of habit. Neural circuits that fire together wire together, meaning the more we think a certain thought, the stronger that neural pathway becomes, making it easier for the brain to default to that thought in the future.'* In other words, our repeated thoughts don't just float in and out—they create well-worn paths in our brains, shaping how we see ourselves and the world. If we constantly tell ourselves we're not enough, that belief strengthens. But the incredible thing is, we have the power to rewrite the script. By consciously choosing to shift our self-talk—replacing doubt with encouragement, fear with possibility—we can reshape those neural pathways and build a mindset that supports us instead of limits us.

Our thoughts don't just exist in isolation; they come wrapped in emotion. The stronger the feeling is attached to a thought, the more likely it is to stick. Fear, shame, joy, pride—these emotions turn fleeting thoughts into deeply held beliefs. If we try something new and fail, embarrassment can latch onto the thought *'I'm not capable,'* making it feel like an undeniable truth rather than just a single moment of struggle. And once a belief takes hold, our brains go to work proving it right. This is confirmation bias in action—where we unconsciously filter the world through the lens of what we already believe.

If we tell ourselves *'I'm unworthy of love,'* we'll gather every rejection, every moment of loneliness as proof, while overlooking the times we were embraced, valued, and deeply seen. But the good news? The same process works in our favor when we choose to shift our thinking to thoughts like *'I am resilient,' 'I deserve kindness,'* or *'I am capable of growth.'* When we pair those positive thoughts with moments of pride, joy, and gratitude, our brains start collecting proof of those truths instead. We begin noticing our small victories, the people who support us, and the progress we're making. When we attach *confidence* to our courage, *excitement* to new opportunities, and *self-compassion* to our missteps, we rewire our minds to see possibility instead of limitation. Our thoughts hold power, but we get to choose which ones we let take root.

From childhood, I had a deeply rooted fear of public speaking. Early on, it was a lack of confidence. However, after my caregiving journey, it became more than a lack of confidence. I had chronicled Peter and my Alzheimer's journey on Facebook, sharing with the world very openly and honestly what Alzheimer's looks like. While the feedback was encouraging and my book, *Oh Hello Alzheimer's*, continues to be very popular, when I began to speak in public as an expert, I suffered from impostor syndrome. If I wanted to continue motivating and inspiring others, I needed to manage my self-doubt.

Imposter Syndrome is the persistent feeling that you're not as capable or competent as others perceive you to be, despite evidence of your skills, achievements, or success. It often comes with self-doubt and downplaying your achievements, believing they're not as impressive as others think. Overcoming imposter syndrome takes practice, self-awareness, and intentional mindset shifts. For the most part, I've tackled the impostor beast and now realize my accomplishments are real and earned. Overcoming imposter syndrome isn't about eliminating self-doubt entirely; it's about recognizing it for what it is and not letting it hold you back. Here are some ways to quiet that inner critic and step fully into your confidence:

1. Call It Out – The first step is simply recognizing when impostor syndrome is creeping in. You're not alone in feeling this way, and acknowledging it takes away some of its power.

2. Flip the Script – When you catch yourself thinking, *I don't deserve this* or *I just got lucky*, challenge that thought. Reframe it with *I worked hard for this* or *My skills and effort got me here.*

3. Keep a Confidence Log – Write down wins, compliments, and moments that made you proud. When doubt creeps in, revisit it. You have proof that you're capable—sometimes you just need a reminder.

4. Say It Out Loud – Imposter syndrome thrives in silence. Share your feelings with trusted friends, mentors, or colleagues. You'll probably be surprised how many successful people have felt the same way.

5. Stay in Your Lane – Comparison is the fastest way to feel like you're falling short. Focus on your own growth, your own strengths, and your own progress instead of measuring yourself against someone else's highlight reel.

6. Ditch Perfectionism – No one has it all figured out. Making mistakes doesn't mean you're not good enough—it means you're learning and growing.

7. Take Action Anyway – You don't have to feel 100% ready to go for something. Confidence often comes from doing, not waiting until you feel "good enough."

8. Recognize Your Impact – Think about the people you've helped, the difference you've made, and the value you bring. Your work, your words, and your presence matter more than you probably give yourself credit for.

9. Get Support When You Need It – If impostor syndrome is holding you back in a big way, consider talking to a coach or therapist. There's no shame in getting guidance to shift your mindset.

You are more capable and worthy than your doubts would have you believe. The more you challenge those impostor thoughts, the more natural it will feel to own your success. A sense of pride is much more rewarding than a sense of doubt. Acknowledge your hard work, skills, and earned outcomes.

Giving ourselves grace rather than criticizing ourselves highlights self-care. Humor is a terrific tool for allowing us to move forward with ease, letting go of embarrassment. "Woopsie! That's not how I intended that to go. Practice makes perfect, let's try that again!" instead of "How embarrassing. I knew I wouldn't be able to do it." That negative self-talk harbors the feeling of embarrassment, creating a rooted, false belief of unworthiness.

We are constantly receiving messages from those around us—family, friends, society—and these messages can deeply shape what we believe about ourselves. Whether it's a comment from a loved one or a message from the world around us, the words we hear most often can stick. If someone repeatedly tells us *"You're too sensitive,"* or *"You're not smart enough,"* it's easy to internalize those words and start believing them as truth. Over time, those external validations become a part of how we see ourselves, shaping our thoughts and actions.

But it doesn't stop there. These external messages merge with our internal thoughts and create habits of thinking that form our identity. If we constantly tell ourselves *"I'm not creative,"* we may avoid creative endeavors, further solidifying the belief that creativity isn't for us. Our beliefs start to define who we are, how we act, and how we approach the world.

The good news is that negative self-limiting beliefs aren't permanent. They're not hardwired into our brains—they're just habits of thinking. By consciously questioning the thoughts that no longer serve us and choosing new, empowering ones, we can shift our mindset and identity. For example, instead of thinking *"I'm not good at public speaking,"* we can shift to *"I am learning to be a confident speaker."* When we actively reinforce these new beliefs with action, they begin to take root and become a part of who we are. We are not stuck with our old beliefs. We can change the narrative and create a new, more supportive version of ourselves.

Sometimes, the hardest part isn't the change itself, it's the resistance to it. We can get so attached to the familiar, even when it doesn't serve us anymore. It feels safer to stay in the comfort of old beliefs and patterns, even if those beliefs hold us back. It's like the brain is telling us, "This is what we know, so let's stick with it." But here's the truth: change doesn't have to feel scary. It can be a process of stepping into something new with grace and curiosity, knowing that we are always growing, always evolving.

Believing in ourselves is the key to unlocking that growth. It's about choosing to step into the unknown, even when it feels uncertain. It's giving ourselves permission to say, "I can do this," and knowing that with each small step forward, we're cultivating a belief in our own abilities. The more we choose to nurture those positive, empowering beliefs, the more they'll take root and shape who we are. So, let's lean into change, not with fear, but with open arms, trusting that each shift brings us closer to the version of ourselves we're meant to be.

Questions to ponder:

1. Can you embrace change instead of resisting it, for self-growth?

2. Think of a recent situation where you felt self-doubt or fear—how could shifting your self-talk have changed your response or perspective?

3. How can you become more aware of the external messages that may be shaping your beliefs, and what new narrative can you choose to embrace instead?

CHAPTER TEN

Self-Compliments Shape Self-Worth

How do compliments affect our self-talk? Compliments hold incredible power—not just because they make us feel good in the moment, but because they can also deeply influence how we see ourselves and how we engage with the world. When someone gives us a genuine compliment, it can act like a mirror, reflecting to us qualities or strengths we might not have fully recognized in ourselves. This external recognition can validate what we may be doubting internally. It's a form of positive reinforcement that aligns with our self-talk, gently nudging us to see ourselves in a more favorable light.

If you're constantly telling yourself, "I'm not good enough," but someone you trust or admire tells you, "You're so thoughtful," that compliment doesn't just brighten your day—it shifts your internal narrative, even if just a little. It adds weight to the positive thought, giving it more credibility and creating a ripple effect. When we receive compliments, especially when they come from a place of genuine care or respect, they serve as a catalyst for positive self-talk. They remind us of the qualities we may have forgotten or taken for granted, which then helps us to reinforce those same qualities in ourselves.

In terms of community influence, compliments also play a significant role in building trust and fostering connections. The simple act of giving someone a sincere compliment creates a moment of validation and belonging. When we offer compliments to others, we're not just lifting them up; we're also contributing to the shared energy of the community. This creates a positive feedback loop—people feel good, they feel seen, and they are more likely to extend the same kindness to others, amplifying the sense of support and positivity within the group. When we recognize the value in each other and verbalize it, we're not only reinforcing their sense of self-worth, but we're also strengthening the bonds of the community.

In both self-talk and community influence, compliments have the power to reshape how we see ourselves and others. They help to replace self-doubt with self-acceptance, reminding us that we are worthy of appreciation and recognition. As we give and receive compliments, we contribute to a culture of encouragement and support, ultimately elevating both our own self-image and the collective spirit of the community.

Accepting compliments with grace can be a challenge for many people, especially if you're not used to receiving positive attention or praise. It often feels more comfortable to deflect, downplay, or minimize compliments, but doing so can unintentionally diminish the value of the acknowledgment.

Accepting compliments can be such a challenge for a few reasons. A lot of it comes down to our internal beliefs about ourselves and our worth, as well as how we've been socialized.

For many people, there's a fear of coming across as arrogant or self-centered. We've been taught to be modest, to downplay our accomplishments, or to avoid drawing attention to ourselves. So, when someone compliments us, our immediate response might be to deflect, because we don't want to seem like we're bragging or taking credit.

Another reason is the tendency toward self-doubt or impostor syndrome. If you're already questioning whether you deserve success or praise, it can feel uncomfortable to accept a compliment. You might feel like you're being "found out" or that the compliment doesn't truly reflect your worth, which can lead to a knee-jerk response of dismissing or minimizing it.

There's also the idea of perfectionism. Many people are conditioned to believe that anything less than perfection isn't worthy of praise. If we don't feel like we've reached the pinnacle of success, we may feel unworthy of compliments, even if what we've done is impressive.

Finally, some people struggle to accept compliments because they've simply never been taught how to. If we didn't grow up in an environment where positive reinforcement or expressions of appreciation were common, it can be hard to internalize and accept that kind of feedback later in life.

When you receive a compliment, try to simply say "thank you." It sounds simple, but allowing yourself to fully accept the recognition without brushing it off allows you to honor the truth in the compliment. It's a moment to embrace positive feedback without attaching any feelings of guilt or self-doubt. Remember, the person giving the compliment is sharing their genuine appreciation, and by graciously accepting it, you're acknowledging their kindness and the truth in what they're saying.

Sometimes, accepting compliments with grace also means letting go of the need to qualify or explain yourself. For example, if someone praises your hard work, you don't need to respond with, "It was nothing," or "I just got lucky." Instead, acknowledge the compliment with humility and confidence. You earned it, and it's okay to accept that.

The more we accept compliments with grace, the more we allow ourselves to receive positive energy and the recognition we deserve. It's an act of self-compassion, reminding ourselves that we're worthy of acknowledgment.

Complimenting yourself is a powerful practice that can have a profound impact on your mental, emotional, and even physical well-being. When you compliment yourself, you're engaging in an act of self-recognition and self-affirmation, which helps to reinforce a positive self-image. Complimenting yourself is a form of self-love. It allows you to acknowledge your own value, regardless of external validation. By regularly affirming your positive traits, achievements, and qualities, you slowly begin to internalize those compliments and reinforce a healthier self-image.

Over time, this increases your confidence and self-worth, making it easier to approach challenges with a positive attitude. Self-compliments work hand-in-hand with positive self-talk. Instead of criticizing or doubting yourself, complimenting yourself helps shift your internal dialogue from negative to supportive. For example, instead of thinking "I messed up again," you can say "I did my best and handled the situation as well as I could." This shift in mindset helps build resilience, as you're acknowledging that setbacks don't define you, but are opportunities to grow.

Many of us have been conditioned to focus on our flaws or shortcomings. By complimenting yourself regularly, you counterbalance that tendency toward self-criticism with kindness and acceptance. This helps reduce the inner critic's grip, allowing you to embrace imperfections with more compassion and less judgment. Complimenting yourself requires you to pause and reflect on your positive qualities, achievements, and progress. This practice cultivates a deeper awareness of your strengths, talents, and growth, which can often be overlooked in the busyness of life. By actively noticing and appreciating your own worth, you foster a sense of gratitude for yourself and your journey.

For example, after baking something new, you could say to yourself, "That turned out great! I'm a good baker!" Or perhaps you knit. When you've tried a new stitch or finished a new pattern, you could tell yourself, "I'm getting better and better at knitting."

When you take the time to compliment yourself for the small wins, you celebrate progress instead of focusing only on the end goal. This sense of accomplishment, even in the smallest things, motivates you to keep going. It encourages you to keep pushing forward with a sense of pride, knowing that you're making strides, regardless of the challenges that may arise. Over time, self-compliments can reshape your inner narrative, helping you break free from limiting beliefs or negative self-perceptions. Instead of being stuck in the cycle of "I'm not good enough" or "I'll never succeed," complimenting yourself allows you to change the story you tell about yourself. You begin to see yourself as capable, worthy, and deserving of success and happiness.

By making self-complimenting a regular practice, you begin to shift from seeking external validation to finding value and worth within yourself. It's an empowering way to honor who you are and the journey you're on, fostering a deeper sense of self-love and acceptance.

Questions to ponder:

1. Can you take advantage of opportunities to compliment others after reflecting on the benefits of a compliment?

2. How can you start noticing the small victories and moments of progress in your life to reinforce positive self-belief?

3. Moving forward, could you say "Thank you" and receive a compliment with grace? You deserve it

CHAPTER ELEVEN

Daily Practices to Reinforce Positive Self-Talk

When we start practicing new ways of thinking, it's important to remember that growth isn't a straight line. It takes time. Just like learning any new skill, whether it's playing an instrument or picking up a new hobby, changing the way we think requires patience and consistency. You won't wake up one day and suddenly have a completely positive inner dialogue, and that's okay. The key is practicing, day by day, knowing that perfection isn't the goal—progress is.

Allow yourself grace on the days when those old negative thoughts try to creep in. It's natural to feel frustrated or discouraged when things don't seem to shift as quickly as you'd like. But rather than judging yourself for slipping back into old patterns, gently guide yourself back. Remind yourself that it's okay to have moments of struggle and that each moment is an opportunity to practice again. The more you practice self-compassion, the more you'll begin to see it as part of the growth process.

The beauty of giving yourself grace is that it removes the pressure of perfection. It gives you permission to stumble and rise again without guilt or shame. In doing so, you create a safe space for growth to happen. Change is uncomfortable, but when we approach it with kindness, it becomes much easier to navigate. You're learning to reshape your thoughts, and that takes time, but every positive shift, no matter how small, is a step forward.

Implementing daily practices can help to reinforce positive thinking. For years I've made it a consistent habit to practice positive affirmations, meditation, and gratitude. I start every day with 20-30 minutes before even putting my feet on the floor. It's a sure way to start the day off in a positive mindset.

I'm very selective about who I spend my time with and how they influence me. The people I choose to spend my time with make me laugh, teach me, soothe me, lift me, and inspire me. Being selective supports my values and keeps me positive. Consider incorporating some of these practices as you transform your thinking.

- Starting your day with mantras or affirmations can rewire negative thought patterns. "My voice matters," or "I am enough," or "I trust myself to make the right choices."
- Practicing gratitude is a powerful tool to shape your thoughts. Instead of "I should be better," shift that criticizing voice to one of self-appreciation, "I am grateful for how far I've come."
- Consider the thoughts you tell yourself. Would you say them to your best friend, partner, or children? Imagine talking to your younger self.

What would you say? Practice speaking to yourself with the same kindness you speak to others.

- Take a few minutes each day to reflect on your strengths and what you're proud of. This could be anything from a skill you've honed to an act of kindness you performed. Recognizing your strengths not only affirms your capabilities but also reinforces the positive belief that you are enough, just as you are.

- Visualization is such a simple but powerful practice for shaping the mindset you want. Take just a few moments each day to close your eyes and imagine yourself succeeding. Picture how it feels to be confident, to speak up with ease, and to approach any challenge with a positive attitude. When you visualize yourself winning, you're literally training your brain to believe it's possible. This practice is especially helpful when you're about to face something challenging— just take a moment to picture yourself handling it calmly, with confidence, and grace. It's a small shift, but it makes a big difference!

- Journaling can be a helpful way to strengthen your practice. By writing down positive thoughts, affirmations, and mantras you can easily refer to and track your positive thoughts. Writing down scenes from visualizing can reinforce those images.

- Daily self-kindness practices can be as simple as taking a moment to savor a cup of tea, walking in nature, or indulging in a hobby that brings you joy. When we take time for these small acts of care, we send a message to ourselves that we deserve love and attention. These moments of care and kindness can act as powerful reminders of our worth and can shift our self-talk in a more positive direction. Remember, self-talk isn't just about words, it's about how we treat ourselves in everyday actions, too.

- Surrounding yourself with a positive community creates mutual empowerment. The people we spend time with don't just influence our actions, they shape our inner dialogue. When we're around people who lift us up, we start to internalize that same encouragement. We begin to see ourselves through a kinder, more capable lens.

- On the flip side, if we're constantly surrounded by negativity or doubt, those voices can creep into our own thoughts, making us question our worth. Choosing a community that reinforces positivity and support isn't just good for the soul—it rewires the way we speak to ourselves, helping us build confidence, resilience, and a deep belief in our own values.

The world is full of voices telling us who we should be, what we should do, and how we should feel about ourselves. But as Jay Shetty, British podcaster, said, *'No one's voice should carry more weight than your own.'* The way we talk to ourselves matters—it shapes our confidence, our choices, and how we show up in the world. When we stop looking outside for validation and start trusting our own voice, we take back our power. The more we affirm our worth from within, the less we rely on anyone else to define it for us.

Questions to ponder:

1. What is one daily practice you can begin to improve your self-talk?

2. What are some signs to look for in your communities to evaluate whether they are positive or negative?

3. Can you give yourself grace during your practice, knowing that growth takes time and perfection isn't the goal, progress is.

CHAPTER TWELVE

Reclaiming My Identity

When I walked out the front door days after Peter's death I stopped abruptly. It felt as though I had forgotten something. You know the feeling. I had my keys and my purse, and I decided I had not forgotten anything physical. What I had forgotten was my identity. Over the course of our Alzheimer's journey, I morphed into a new person. Slowly, the parts of me I wanted to hold on to vanished and were replaced by the parts of me that Peter needed.

I hadn't felt the freedom of simply walking out the front door in years. But that day, I just got ready, slipped on my shoes, grabbed my purse, and climbed into the car; no overthinking, no extra steps. Such a simple act, yet an absolute luxury compared to just weeks before, when even the smallest outing required immense preparation. Hiring and scheduling a professional caregiver was one thing—trusting that they would provide the care Peter needed was another. Going over care instructions while I was away, I worried, had I forgotten anything? Had I properly familiarized them with Peter's behaviors and needs.

The anxiety of leaving him made it hard to feel any real sense of freedom. I knew he would be agitated and anxious from the moment I left until I returned, and I constantly worried whether the caregiver would handle him with the care and patience he deserved. I hoped his agitation wouldn't escalate into combativeness. Even when I was away from home, my mind never truly left.

During that time, I had become a full-time caregiver. While I was still considered Peter's wife, I felt more like his mother. I adored being a mother to my children and stepchildren, but felt as though I was relying more on them for support than providing any support to them. I did not feel like the engaged grandmother I wanted to be. Consumed by caregiving, I had little time to even consider myself a good friend to anyone. There was little time for enjoying my own interests, and I no longer considered myself a hiker, reader, traveler, foodie, or avid gardener. I became who I needed to be, but that person no longer served me.

And then, like many of my readers, my husband passed away. I was no longer a caregiver, and in that moment of profound loss, I stepped into a new role—one I never anticipated, but had to embrace.

I remember feeling the revelation of "Oh my God, I'm a widow!" The label felt dark and hopeless, as though I would never feel joy or excitement or anticipation again. I decided immediately that I was not subscribing to that stereotype. I did not want to conform to the label of survivor either; I had always been a thriver. Though I wasn't doing much thriving yet, I would be.

I have always loved the feeling of freedom, but after being tethered for years, it felt a bit overwhelming, too. Like a bobbing balloon filled with helium held only by a small hand, I didn't feel secure. I was frightened of being untethered and some days wanted the comfort and discomfort of being a caregiver. Evaluating my identity felt both intimidating and freeing. Who was I before Alzheimer's? It was hard for me to remember, so instead I asked myself, "What activities did I participate in before?" The answers popped into my head, and I felt energized. Traveling, hiking, gardening, reading, meditating, working, cooking, self-care, and spending time with my family were all things that had needed to be put on hold. Which of these did I want to resurrect? Which did I want to relinquish?

I relied on my internal guidance system to reunite me with the things that felt good and discard those that didn't. After years of caregiving, I now had the opportunity to make choices based on my own desires rather than obligations. Deciding what to keep and what to release helped me regain a sense of control over my life. Some activities no longer aligned with who I wanted to become. Letting go of them allowed me to embrace new interests and opportunities that reflected my evolving identity. I was fortunate that I had the choice of whether or not to go back to a traditional career. I decided I did not and created my own business, writing, speaking, and consulting. This new part of my identity was filled with purpose as I was supporting and educating families and professionals.

I was not tethered to a boss or corporation and had the freedom to do as little or as much as I wanted. It was exciting to use my experiences to create projects that help others. Learning these new skills provided stimulation I had not felt for some time. By relinquishing the role of employee, I made space for this exciting new change. Instead of asking, "Who was I?' I began asking, 'Who am I?' I'm an author, speaker, consultant, and business owner!

My physical body hadn't been well cared for. I'd neither had the time nor the motivation, and so exercise and healthy eating slipped into neglect. It was time to reengage and prioritize my health. Hiking and gardening had always been two of my favorite activities. Both brought me peace and helped quiet my busy mind. When my hands are planting or delicately pruning, my need to nurture is fulfilled. Hiking, on the other hand, gets me into the woods to explore and appreciate the wonders that surround us.

Both hiking and gardening are huge anxiety and stress reducers for me. I see them as acts of self-care, nurturing both my body and my mind. Hiking helps build my endurance and cardiovascular health, while gardening promotes flexibility and dexterity, two things that become even more important as I get older. Reuniting with these two familiar hobbies brought me an incredible sense of joy! Who am I? I'm a hiker and avid gardener!

We resumed family dinners and gatherings. Guilt plagued me as I knew there were gaps in my knowledge about what was happening in my children's lives. I had been too occupied to be intentional and present in our conversations. I had missed things that were important to them as I became less and less involved during those caregiving years. It was delicious reconnecting and practicing that intentional presence once again. I loved immersing myself back into their lives as I had in the past. Sonny had a new baby brother, and playdates with both the boys soon resumed. Who am I? I'm an involved Mom and Gramma!

The truest of friends were solidly supportive during my journey with Alzheimer's. Whether they offered emotional care through phone conversations, brought meals, or provided hands-on help, their support was unwavering. The challenge was that I couldn't reciprocate in the same way, and that left me with a sense of guilt. I felt as though I wasn't able to give back to the people who had given me so much during such a difficult time. My friendships felt one-sided, and it was time to equalize that balance.

Being able to show up for my friends after Peter's death helped me release that guilt and replace it with gratitude and appreciation for the relationships that sustained me during tough times. The more time I spent with my closest friends, the better I felt. By re-engaging and being present with my friends, I rebuilt a sense of mutual connection and balance. This strengthened my support network and gave me a sense of belonging, which was essential for my emotional healing. By being genuinely interested and present, the natural flow of giving and receiving was restored. Who am I? I'm a good friend!

Peter and I used to travel extensively, and I missed exploring new places and experiencing new things. I decided it was important to me and booked a trip to Clearwater Beach, Florida. Just me. I had never traveled alone before, except for driving to Pennsylvania to visit my family. It was invigorating and empowering, and I was immediately hooked! Walking the beaches, meeting new people by the pool, and exploring the town introduced me to the confident, independent woman I had forgotten! Before Peter and I got married, I did a lot of things alone and loved that independence. Who am I? I'm a confident, independent woman and traveler!

While I was a caregiver, my mind was consumed with worry, and even if I tried to read a book or meditate, my mind would wander. I longed to immerse myself in a good book and surrender myself to the art of meditation. I decided to make both a daily practice. Practicing meditation has helped to quiet my mind and taught me to redirect my thoughts when they turn to worrying about the future or thinking about the past. I view reading as a form of meditation. My mind is calm and uncluttered. When I plunge myself into a book, I'm present in the story or lessons. When I'm reading or meditating, I'm physically calm, which is restorative for my body. Often, I'll meditate under a blanket on the couch after hiking, and then read a few chapters. I've also been known to wake up on the couch, surprised after an unplanned nap! Who am I? I'm an intentional reader and meditator!

I have embraced reinvention while honoring who I used to be. Releasing the things that no longer served me created space to challenge myself to try new things. Practicing self-compassion along the way was vital. Healing those feelings of guilt for neglecting my family and friends took time and intentional reciprocation. Letting go of social stigmas helped me to grow and heal more quickly into the person I am becoming. I am a widow, and I survived something terrible. I will always grieve Peter, but it doesn't define who I am. I am at peace with who I've become, the challenges I've overcome to get here, and the future me I haven't met yet!

Questions to ponder:

1. Are there new things you want to try, but have been afraid to? What's stopping you?

2. If you evaluated your identity, are there things you would like to relinquish?

3. Are you harboring guilt in any relationships? Are there simple actions you could take to remedy the situation?

CHAPTER THIRTEEN

Forgiveness, a Gift to Yourself

Forgiveness isn't just something we offer others; it's a gift to ourselves. When we hold onto resentment, we carry the weight of past pain like a heavy backpack, draining our energy and clouding our perspective. Letting go of that burden doesn't mean condoning what happened or pretending it didn't hurt; it means choosing peace over pain. It's about freeing ourselves from the grip of old wounds so we can move forward with clarity, strength, and an open heart. Whether we're forgiving others or ourselves, the act of releasing anger, guilt, or disappointment allows us to reclaim our joy and emotional well-being.

As a caregiver, I often felt the salty unfairness of what my life had become. Losing my husband wasn't fair, and I wanted someone to blame. Alzheimer's introduced her ugly face when Peter and I were enjoying life to the fullest. As a couple, we had plans and dreams for our future together. Our careers were secure, and we were thriving individually. Our marriage was beautifully orchestrated with excitement, romance, and celebration. We were gliding easily toward our golden years, anticipating early retirement at 60. Our dream became a nightmare when Peter was diagnosed at 53. Peter died four years short of our goal.

The space between diagnosis and death was shattering, as I've detailed in my book *Oh, Hello Alzheimer's*. Who was to blame? Where could I place this resentment? There was no one to blame, and my newfound radical acceptance helped me navigate the beauty of forgiveness. Rather than carrying the identity of a victim, I easily relinquished any resentment I may have felt, trading it for peace.

Caregiving is relentless. Even the most patient and experienced caregiver will lose their temper, make imperfect choices, and act in ways they never imagined. It's exhausting, unpredictable, and, at times, overwhelming. But giving ourselves grace—choosing to release the guilt we carry—can be one of the most empowering things we do. Acknowledging our own humanity, recognizing that we're doing the best we can, and practicing self-compassion isn't just kindness, it's a necessity. We are our own harshest critics, holding ourselves to impossible standards. Learning to extend grace to ourselves as we would a friend is an essential part of personal growth.

Forgiveness is a gift we give ourselves. Letting go of resentment brings healing, peace, and a deep sense of relief. The weight of holding onto anger or guilt is heavy, draining our energy, and adding to our stress. But we always have a choice— to release it, to free ourselves, and to move forward with a lighter heart. Forgiveness means carrying love and understanding forward instead of enduring unresolved pain.

Society is full of 'shoulds.' We're told how things *should* go, how we *should* act, and how we *should* respond. But life doesn't work that way. Clinging to what *should* have been, how someone *should* have treated us, or how we *should* have handled a situation, only keeps us stuck in frustration and disappointment. The past won't change, no matter how much we replay it.

The phrase "Stop shoulding on yourself" is often attributed to psychologist Albert Ellis, the founder of Rational Emotive Behavior Therapy (REBT). Ellis used this phrase to describe the unhealthy habit of imposing rigid expectations on ourselves and others, leading to guilt, frustration, and stress. Ellis discussed the concept in his book, *A Guide to Rational Living* (1975), where he emphasized that replacing 'should' statements with more flexible, self-compassionate language can lead to better emotional well-being.

Forgiveness gives us the power to let go of those expectations and accept what *is* instead of staying trapped in what we wish had been. It doesn't mean excusing hurtful actions or pretending things were fine when they weren't. It means choosing peace over resentment, growth over holding grudges. It's a decision to release the weight of 'should' and make space for something lighter, something better.

Stubbornness can really get in the way of forgiveness. It's that inner voice that says, "I'm right, and they're wrong," or "I shouldn't have to let go." It digs in its heels and holds onto the idea that someone else needs to be the first to change, apologize, or admit fault before we can move forward. The problem with stubbornness is that it can keep us stuck in a loop of frustration and resentment just to prove a point. We end up carrying around all this emotional weight, thinking we're protecting ourselves when, in reality, it's just holding us back from peace. Letting go of that stubborn need to be right, or to have things play out exactly how we think they should, opens up the space for healing and release. Forgiveness isn't about condoning what happened; it's about setting ourselves free from the past.

Forgiveness reminds us that people are complicated, and most of us are doing the best we can with what we know. When we embrace compassion, we release ourselves from the need to judge and punish. The need to keep score and practice tit-for-tat dissipates. Many people see forgiveness as "letting someone off the hook," when, in reality, it's an act of courage. It takes courage and strength to choose peace over bitterness and to reclaim our own power instead of staying trapped in anger. Forgiveness humbles us, reminding us that peace matters more than pride.

A long-term grudge is an emotional weight that builds over time, draining your energy and clouding your perspective. The longer you hold onto it, the more space it takes up in your mind, influencing your thoughts, emotions, and even your well-being. It can create tension, resentment, and stress, often affecting you far more than the person you're holding it against. Holding onto a grudge for months or years means you're not just holding on to a memory but to all the negative feelings associated with it: anger, betrayal, hurt, and resentment. It's a constant drain on your emotional energy, and over time, it can affect your mental and even physical well-being.

What's tricky about long-term grudges is that they often become a part of our identity. We start to define ourselves by the wrongs done to us, and it becomes easy to keep rehashing the story in our minds, justifying the grudge. But the longer we hold onto it, the more it robs us of our peace and joy, making it harder to move forward. It can impact relationships, clouding our ability to trust or fully embrace others, or even see them clearly without the filter of past pain.

Forgiveness isn't about telling someone they were right or excusing their actions—it's about freeing ourselves from the grip of that anger. It's a process, but when we choose to let go of a long-term grudge, we stop carrying around all that emotional baggage. We give ourselves the chance to heal, grow, and move on with less weight on our shoulders. And while it can be tough to break free from old resentments, it opens the door to more peace, freedom, and emotional lightness.

Forgiveness isn't expecting an apology; it's unconditional. The truth is, you don't need an apology to heal. Forgiveness and emotional freedom come from within, not from waiting for someone else to fix what they've done. When you choose to forgive, it's about letting go of the power that person or that situation has over you. While an apology would certainly help, you have the ability to heal and move forward without it. Choosing to forgive doesn't mean you condone the behavior or that you're saying everything is okay, but rather that you're making peace with it for your own well-being.

If you do get the apology you've been waiting for, that's a wonderful bonus, but remember, your healing doesn't have to be dependent on it. You deserve peace regardless of what others do. Yes, true forgiveness is unconditional; it's a gift you give yourself, not something that depends on whether the other person acknowledges their wrongdoing or apologizes. If forgiveness were conditional, it would mean your healing and peace are in someone else's hands, and that's a lot of power to give away.

Forgiveness doesn't mean forgetting, excusing, or allowing harmful behavior to continue. It simply means you're releasing the emotional hold that resentment has over you. It's about choosing peace over pain, freedom over bitterness. You can forgive and still maintain boundaries. You can forgive and still decide that certain people or situations don't belong in your life.

Questions to ponder:

1. How can forgiveness bring peace to a situation in your life?

2. Have you been 'shoulding on yourself,' causing anxiety and stress?

3. Can you forgive someone unconditionally without expecting an apology?

CHAPTER FOURTEEN

Pruning Your Circle for Growth

Not everyone deserves unlimited access to you. Your time, energy, wisdom, and compassion are valuable, and protecting them is essential for your well-being. Balance ensures that relationships are built on mutual respect. It's okay to give generously, but not endlessly. When that balance is off, it's easy to feel drained or even taken advantage of, which can lead to resentment.

This applies to both relationships and conversations. If someone constantly talks about themselves without ever showing interest in you, it starts to feel like a one-sided exchange, a time suck. For any relationship or conversation to feel fulfilling and balanced, both people need to feel seen and valued. If someone is blathering on and on, the listener tends to lose interest and search for an exit. Conversely, when someone shows genuine interest and asks questions, the listener feels engaged and valued. I'll explore this more in a future chapter on dating, but one of my core rules applies here as well: In relationships, both parties need to be interesting and be interested.

I have a long-time friend named Peter Z. From the day I met Peter, I have openly expressed what I consider to be his best characteristic. When I'm having a conversation with Peter, he is present. His eyes are locked in, and he's very interested in hearing the answers to the questions he's asking. His body leans toward me. He doesn't interrupt, which is something I'm constantly trying to improve. Peter asks follow-up questions and shows genuine interest. He's an outstanding conversationalist. Whenever I spend time with Peter, I feel seen and heard, and our friendship is strengthened even though we don't spend a lot of time together. I strive to offer my friendships this same level of presence.

Peter Z sets some important boundaries. Peter's presence in conversation isn't just about being engaged; it's also about the boundaries he naturally upholds. He doesn't allow distractions to pull him away; when he's talking to someone, he's not glancing at his phone or scanning the room. He also respects the flow of a conversation, he listens fully rather than waiting for his turn to speak, and he never dominates the discussion. Peter makes it clear that his time and energy are valuable, and he chooses to invest them in meaningful, reciprocal conversations. His boundaries don't push people away; they invite the right kind of connection.

By setting boundaries clearly and consistently, we teach people how to treat us. By showing others we value ourselves and our well-being, we set standards for how people engage with us. Our actions, reactions, and boundaries set the tone for how we want to be treated, whether consciously or unconsciously. In the case of conversations with Peter, I wouldn't dare pick up my phone or allow myself to be distracted. Peter taught me how to treat him through his example of how he treats me.

If we tolerate behavior that disrespects us, it can signal to the person that this behavior is acceptable. If we stand up for ourselves and speak up when something bothers us, we reinforce that disrespect will not be tolerated. Disrespect can show up in many forms, some subtle and some more obvious.

In friendships and relationships:

- Interrupting constantly – Showing little regard for your thoughts or contributions.
- One-sided conversations – Talking only about themselves and not asking about you.
- Dismissing your feelings – Saying things like, "You're overreacting." or "That's not a big deal."
- Breaking commitments – Repeatedly canceling plans last minute without considering your time.
- Taking advantage of kindness – Always expecting favors but never offering support in return.

At work:

- Ignoring contributions – Not acknowledging your ideas or taking credit for your work.
- Not valuing your input – Speaking over you in meetings.
- Microaggressions or condescension – Saying things like, "Oh, that's cute" when you present an idea.
- Disregarding your time – Sending late-night emails and expecting an immediate response.

In family dynamics:

- Making you the family problem solver – Expecting you to fix everything without considering your needs.
- Belittling your choices – Criticizing your career, relationships, or parenting style.
- Guilt-tripping – Saying things like, "If you really cared, you'd do this for me."
- Invalidating your experiences – Responding with, "That never happened," or "You're too sensitive."

In romantic relationships:

- Lack of appreciation – Never acknowledging your efforts or saying thank you.
- Not respecting your boundaries – Pushing you to do things you're uncomfortable with.
- Silent treatment as punishment – Withholding affection or communication instead of addressing issues.
- Making jokes at your expense – Disguising insults as humor and saying, "Relax, I was just kidding."

In social settings and everyday life:

- Ignoring basic social etiquette – Cutting in line.
- Being habitually late – Disrespecting your time and effort.
- Talking down to service workers – Treating people as "less than."
- Ignoring personal space – Invading your boundaries physically or emotionally.

Disrespect is often about a lack of consideration, empathy, or acknowledgment of another person's worth. Recognizing it is the first step in setting boundaries and ensuring you're surrounded by relationships that uplift rather than drain you.

Relationships should be reciprocal. Take a hard look at your friendships. Do they bring you joy or leave you feeling drained? After spending some time with someone, do you feel uplifted and energized or depleted and exhausted? That simple question can reveal a lot.

Who supports you without conditions? The best relationships don't require you to shrink, overextend, or suppress your needs. They inspire you to be big, grow, and learn. Healthy relationships are easy, and we eagerly anticipate spending time with those we connect with most deeply. Another question to ask yourself when evaluating your friends: do I anticipate spending time with this person with excitement or dread?

Like in gardening, pruning doesn't always mean cutting something off completely. Sometimes, it's about creating space for healthier growth. The same goes for friendships. Spending less time with someone who isn't influencing you in the ways you want can be beneficial. It's okay to create distance without drama; not every friendship needs a big breakup. Sometimes, gradually stepping back is enough. And some friendships are simply seasonal, and that's okay. As we focus on self-growth, it's natural to outgrow certain relationships. People come into our lives for a season, a reason, or a lifetime. Each connection, no matter how long, shapes us in its own way.

You can't give equal energy to everyone, and you shouldn't feel guilty about being selective. If someone consistently makes an effort, meets you halfway, and respects your boundaries, invest in that connection. Lean into relationships that feel mutually beneficial. True friends respect your growth and boundaries and are worth nurturing.

Questions to ponder:

1. When you evaluate your friendships, are there relationships that need to be pruned and some that need to be nourished?

2. Looking through the bullet points of disrespect, are there areas that you could improve to show up more fully in your relationships?

3. What are some boundaries you need to implement in order to facilitate self-growth?

CHAPTER FIFTEEN

Communicating Boundaries with Kindness: Words, Actions, Energy, Silence

Years ago, before I became proficient at setting boundaries, I had a friend with whom I would walk several days a week. We were co-workers, mothers, sisters, and dog owners. We shared a love for the beach and enjoyed brisk morning walks. We had so much in common, and we could have discussed and debated plenty of topics. Unfortunately, that wasn't the dynamic we ended up with.

Our walks would last 45 minutes, and my friend would spend the entire time complaining, finding a negative spin on every situation. She would ask for advice but wouldn't take it. More often than not, she'd talk herself into tears during what should have been a pleasant walk. The experience became overwhelming and uncomfortable—it felt so one-sided. I offered uplifting advice, different positive perspectives, and shared examples from my own experiences. But she seemed unwilling, or perhaps unable, to listen, preferring instead to replay old tapes from her past, as she put it.

Her energy pulled me down rather than lifted me up. I was not as confident about setting boundaries back then, and I allowed myself to continue in a relationship that was not serving me. I felt bad that she seemed so unhappy and wanted to help her. But week after week, the conversations felt the same. It was daunting.

I did little to change the situation. The hope I had and the advice I gave fell on deaf ears. Our relationship organically fizzled out when I changed jobs. Today, I would handle the situation very differently. If I were in that same situation now, I might politely decline the invitation to walk with that friend, creating space to spend time with someone I truly want to be with, rather than feeling obligated to spend time with someone who doesn't contribute to my well-being. I now focus on spending my time in healthy, balanced relationships, not the kind that drain me. I surround myself with people who are both interesting and interested, those who share about themselves and genuinely ask questions about my life. These relationships are about giving and receiving. They leave me feeling uplifted, motivated, and inspired.

Part of building these healthier relationships is recognizing that boundaries don't push people away; they deepen the right connections. Respectful boundaries strengthen relationships by creating clarity and mutual respect. They allow us to show up more honestly, more consistently, and with more energy.

For many of us, especially those who avoid conflict or doubt their own worth, setting boundaries can feel uncomfortable, even selfish. But the truth is, expressing your needs isn't selfish — it's self-respect. Boundaries are not walls; they're bridges that guide others in how to care for you. When you communicate your limits with kindness and clarity, those who value and respect you will honor them. And when they do, your bond grows stronger, not in spite of your boundary, but because of it. Setting boundaries is a form of self-trust, and that trust becomes the foundation for a deeper, healthier connection with others.

And here's something many people don't realize: boundaries don't create conflict, they often prevent it. By clearly expressing what works for you and what doesn't, you reduce misunderstandings, avoid built-up resentment, and minimize the emotional toll of unmet expectations. Boundaries bring peace. They reduce stress, because you're no longer stretching yourself too thin or quietly carrying what you were never meant to hold alone.

Today, if I felt value in the relationship, I would communicate my boundaries more clearly: "I understand you're going through a tough time, and I care about you." A statement like this shows empathy and compassion.

I would be honest about my feelings and say something like, "I've noticed during our walks I often feel drained and overwhelmed by the negativity. It's been hard for me to enjoy our time together because I feel like I'm carrying most of the emotional weight."

Using "I" statements rather than "You" statements keep the conversation focused on my feelings, rather than sounding accusatory. "I've realized that I need more positivity in my relationships, and I'm finding it hard to be around negative conversations all the time."

Speaking with clarity and specificity, "I'd love to continue spending time with you, but I need our conversations to be more supportive and balanced. Can we focus on talking about things that uplift us? Maybe we can still walk but I'd like to talk about more positive things."

Setting firm boundaries without being harsh gives my friend the choice to continue spending time together in a positive way or discontinue our walks. "I really value our friendship, but I need to take care of my emotional health, too. I hope you understand why I need to make some changes to how we spend time together."

Communicating discontent to a friend, especially when setting boundaries, can be unnerving, but its essential for maintaining healthy relationships. Communicating honestly with compassion and empathy is the best way to protect your energy. Without open communication, resentment builds, emotional exhaustion sets in, and the relationship remains unbalanced. More than that, avoiding these conversations can hinder personal growth and keep you stuck in unhealthy patterns. If my friend chose not to continue walking together, I would at least feel peaceful knowing I did what I could to deepen our relationship.

Communicating boundaries clearly can be as simple as punctuation. A period at the end of a sentence. "I'm not available for that." Period. No need to follow up with justification or an explanation. Don't let the silence that could come after your statement make you feel uneasy, let it empower you. Not every boundary needs an explanation. Declining an invitation or request is enough. You don't owe everyone a reason and you shouldn't feel guilty.

Recently, a fellow board member asked me to join a committee she was forming. She was enthusiastic when she ran into me at an event and excitedly explained her committee's goals. "It's only an hour a month, one meeting." In my mind I thought, "I don't care if it's one minute a month, I cannot add one more thing to my schedule." I communicated a bit more delicately, "I'm overextended as it is, and I cannot take on one more thing right now or I won't be doing anything well."

A few minutes earlier I had a robust conversation with a new acquaintance who happens to align perfectly with what my fellow board member was orchestrating. Together we walked over to my new acquaintance, I introduced the women and briefly explained why I was connecting them. I handed over the baton and left the conversation. The women were excited to meet, and a new committee member was born. I felt satisfied that I helped out, but didn't overcommit.

Silence is a powerful communicator. A comma before reacting, a moment of silence can give you just enough time to contemplate your answer. Whether deciding to commit to something or not, or just pausing to react with grace and intentionality instead of emotion. In any instance, a little thoughtfulness can alleviate possible overcommitting or conflict.

Response time can be a potent boundary setter. You don't need to reply to all text messages and emails immediately. Constantly being available and responding to every message right away can be overwhelming and draining. By not replying immediately, you give yourself the space to prioritize what matters most to you, while reinforcing a buffer between your time and someone else's demands.

Energy delivers a mighty message. Whether you're projecting enthusiasm or silence, both can deliver a punch. When you show enthusiasm in your interactions, you set a boundary that encourages positivity, respect, and shared energy in relationships, conversations, and activities. Enthusiasm can be a clear signal that you expect conversations and engagements to be uplifting and positive.

On the other hand, using silence as a response to disrespect can be deafening. If someone continues to disregard your boundaries, withdrawing your energy can be a more powerful statement than words. There's power in knowing when to speak and when to let your actions speak for you. Sometimes, silence creates space for the other person to reflect on their behavior and recognize the impact of their actions.

Communicating boundaries with kindness is essential for nurturing healthy, balanced relationships. It's not about pushing people away but creating space for deeper connections with those who respect your needs. By practicing clarity, empathy, and patience, you ensure your boundaries are respected. Silence, response time, and the energy you project all reinforce your standards and protect your emotional well-being. Healthy relationships thrive on mutual respect, and by communicating your boundaries, you invite growth, understanding, and deeper connections. Though it may feel uncomfortable at first, setting boundaries is crucial for protecting your peace and fostering uplifting relationships.

Questions to ponder:

1. Can you effectively communicate and uphold boundaries to support your well-being?

2. What boundary will you focus on setting first?

3. Looking back, can you identify situations where setting a boundary could have been beneficial?

CHAPTER SIXTEEN

Nurturing Relationships for Optimum Growth

Just as a garden needs pruning, relationships need care, attention, and the right environment to grow and thrive. Some connections need more tending, while others flourish effortlessly. When you prioritize the relationships you value most, you naturally invest more energy into the ones that uplift and support you. This intentional focus strengthens those connections and allows them to flourish.

Nurturing relationships through small, meaningful gestures truly makes a difference. These little actions create a lasting impression and reinforce the value of friendship. I love sending greeting cards to my friends to let them know I'm thinking about them and to tell them I'm grateful for their friendship. In the springtime, I'll include a packet of flower seeds as a special touch.

Sending birthday cards is one of my favorite things to do! I've got a box that is organized by month with my friends' and family's birthdates listed. When I find a card just perfect for someone, I file it in the box to mail it later in the year. Who doesn't love to get a surprise card in the mail!

Here are some additional small, thoughtful gestures that can make a big impact on someone's day:

- Random check-in texts. "Hey, I was thinking about you today, let's catch up soon," makes someone feel valued.
- Voice message instead of a text. Sometimes hearing a friend's voice makes all the difference. A heartfelt check-in or funny story adds a personal touch.
- Offering a genuine compliment. Whether it's about their appearance, their resilience, or taste in music, a compliment can make someone's day and boost their self-confidence.
- Sending a funny meme or GIF. A simple, low-effort way to share a laugh or private joke.
- Sharing a good book or article. If you read something that reminds you of them, tell them. "I thought you'd love this!" A gesture like this makes your friend feel seen and heard.

Gestures like these take effort. Relationships that are worthwhile take effort. Ask yourself: Would you want to be friends with you? It's easy to have expectations of others, but true connection happens when we embody the qualities we seek, like kindness, support, reliability, and respect.

I learned this lesson the hard way with my friend Vicki. I value my friendship with Vicki immensely. We have a very easy and natural connection; we can laugh hard together, be serious together, and Vicki supported me through the hardest time in my life. She made the effort, and she showed up.

I was dating someone new, spending most of my energy with Mr. Not-so-right. I was not prioritizing Vicki the way she deserved. I had cancelled lunch plans twice to do something with the new man instead. I was not responding to texts or calls as quickly as I had in the past. This was not like me, and when I realized I was not carrying my weight, I reached out with a text, "Ok. I'm done being a shitty friend. Can you please put me on your calendar?" When I received Vicki's response, I was embarrassed by my behavior.

"Hi. Thought about this text, Lisa…But we are in different lanes on this road of life. However, I still love you. And my reality is that I have two weekend house guests. So, will have to table a date for another time. I do hope you are safe and well. Hugs. V"

I had been pruned! My heart sank, and my anxiety climbed. Vicki had reminded me of her boundaries and friendship requirements. I was humbled and humiliated. I sent a quick response, "I'm sorry I suck! I miss you. I hope you have an amazing couple of weekends. Love you" and then immediately went to the store to buy her a card. To lose my friendship with Vicki would make me very sad. I respected her boundaries and knew I needed to step up and participate more fully in the relationship.

After Vicki received my card, I sent her another text reinforcing how valuable our friendship is to me: "Thank you for making me look in the mirror. I love you immensely. My life is richer with you in it. Thank you for making me realize I haven't been carrying my weight in our relationship. Please know, I'm so very grateful that you are my friend, and I learn so much from you." Our relationship was immediately back on track, and I learned a very valuable lesson about carrying my weight in the relationships I cherish.

In a marriage or partnership, the small daily gestures that nurture connection and joy are imperative. It's often these simple acts of love, appreciation, and understanding that sustain the relationship through the ups and downs. When you consistently nurture your bond with small acts, you create a foundation of trust, joy, and emotional intimacy.

One of the most impactful ways to nurture a relationship is by expressing gratitude daily. Whether it's as simple as saying, "I appreciate you for making dinner tonight," or acknowledging something your partner has done that made your day easier, these small words go a long way. They remind your partner that they are seen, valued, and loved.

Quality time is also vital, especially in the hustle and bustle of life. It's easy to get distracted by responsibilities, but taking intentional moments to connect, like having a conversation over coffee or enjoying a quiet walk, keeps the emotional bond strong. Small moments of undivided attention, like putting down the phone during dinner, can make a huge difference. I like to schedule at least two date nights per month so we can focus entirely on each other without distractions. Typically, we'll linger through dinner at a local restaurant, followed by hanging out at home with no TV. A good dose of quality-focused engagement is a terrific way to connect more deeply and nurture our relationship.

Small, surprise acts of kindness can also fuel the relationship. A thoughtful note, a random "just because" text, or a packet of their favorite snack can show that you're thinking about them. These acts serve as small reminders of love that don't need to be elaborate, just heartfelt.

Another meaningful practice is regularly checking in emotionally. Asking, "How was your day?" and actually listening without distractions shows that you're invested in each other's emotional well-being. These moments of emotional vulnerability bring couples closer, creating a safe space to share both highs and lows.

Physical touch is equally important. Whether it's holding hands, giving a hug, or simply brushing past each other with a gentle touch, physical affection nurtures closeness and provides reassurance. I've found that a good morning kiss, before starting the day, helps us feel more grounded and connected.

Laughter and humor play a significant role in keeping the relationship light and joyful. Sharing jokes, watching funny shows together, or recalling inside jokes can make even the most mundane moments feel special. It's important to enjoy each other's company and not take things too seriously all the time.

Respecting each other's boundaries is crucial for maintaining a healthy dynamic. It's important to understand and honor each other's needs for space or time alone. This shows respect and allows each person to continue growing as individuals while still being connected as a couple.

Understanding and speaking your partner's love language is key. This idea comes from Dr. Gary Chapman's book *The 5 Love Languages*, which identifies five distinct ways people express and receive love: words of affirmation, acts of service, quality time, physical touch, and gifts. When we learn to speak the language that resonates most with our partner, our love becomes more intentional, more effective, and more deeply felt. I remember the first time I realized my partner and I were speaking different love languages—it was a turning point. Once we tuned into each other's way of giving and receiving love, connection became easier, sweeter, and more natural. Even small efforts feel big when they're aligned with what truly speaks to someone's heart.

Finally, ending the day on a positive note can set the tone for the next day. It doesn't matter if it's a brief "I love you" or cuddling before bed. These simple affirmations or quiet moments of togetherness strengthen the emotional bond, leaving you both with a sense of warmth and connection before sleep.

By practicing these small but powerful daily gestures, you can nurture a deeper, more joyful connection in your marriage or partnership. It's not always about the big moments, but about the consistent, small actions that show you care. By cultivating love in the everyday moments, you create a lasting foundation of happiness and support that will carry both of you through life's challenges.

Questions to ponder:

1. Which are the relationships in your life that you want to nurture the most?

2. What are some small gestures that resonate with you and are easy to implement?

3. When you feel disconnected in a relationship or partnership, what steps can you take to feel connected again?

CHAPTER SEVENTEEN

Generosity and Random Acts of Kindness

I frequently take my grandsons to the dollar store to buy them a new toy when they spend the day with me. They take their time, eyes wide open with wonder, carefully studying the shelf of toys as they thoughtfully consider their choice. One day, Liam chose a little plastic wagon, and then he toddled to wait in line at the register, pulling his new find behind him. There was a man ahead of us in line, and the clerk was ringing up his grocery items. Liam and I waited patiently, and when the man gathered the bags he had purchased, he left something on the counter. We had not spoken up until this point, when the man turned to me, pointing to the matchbox car on the counter, he said shyly, "For him."

Liam, being two, did not understand what happened; he only understood that he got a cool new car. But I did. I probably told five or more people about our experience, expressing what a kind gesture that was! One act of kindness has the power to spread farther than we realize. We've all witnessed moments when a simple gesture like holding the door open for someone, picking up the tab for someone, or offering a sincere compliment changes the energy in the room.

The receiver often pays it forward, creating a chain reaction of positivity. After our stop at the dollar store, I drove through the Dunkin' Donuts drive-through for a cup of coffee. Because the man bought Liam a matchbox car, I was inspired to buy the coffee for the person behind me. Kindness is contagious, and when we model it, we inspire others to do the same.

Generosity isn't just about what we give to others; it is about what we give to ourselves in the process. When we show up, whether through time, words, or gestures, we create a ripple effect that can extend far beyond the moment. A small act of thoughtfulness can brighten someone's day, shift their mindset, or even restore their faith in humanity.

Generosity is a two-way street, and science proves what we already feel in our hearts: kindness changes us for the better. Research from the American Psychological Association shows that acts of generosity and kindness benefit both our mental and physical health. Acts of generosity release feel-good chemicals like dopamine and oxytocin, reducing stress and increasing happiness. People feel happier when they spend money on others rather than themselves, and that joy often inspires even more generosity.

One form of generosity, volunteering, has been linked to better overall health in older adults and is even associated with a longer lifespan. Even the smallest acts of kindness can lower stress, boost well-being, and deepen our sense of connection with others. Simply put, giving, in any form, makes us feel more connected, fulfilled, and at peace. When we shift our focus outward and engage in meaningful gestures, it pulls us out of our own struggles and reminds us of the impact we can have on others.

Simply put, giving in any form makes us feel more connected, fulfilled, and at peace. We've all had those fleeting moments where we think, I should reach out to them or send a thank you note. The gap between *intention and action* is often where regrets creep in. We wish we had sent the message, or our self-talk turns to thoughts such as "I'm not very good at reaching out." Closing the gap by following through on that thoughtful idea makes all the difference. If a kind thought enters your mind, act on that thought right away. Send the text, place the order, write the note. The effort is small, but the impact is lasting.

That gap is usually made of tiny hesitations—waiting for the "right moment," searching for perfect words, or assuming someone else will step in—and meanwhile the moment passes. Kindness doesn't need perfect; it needs a nudge. Try shrinking the distance with simple bridges: the ten-second rule (if a generous impulse appears, act within ten seconds), the one-minute rule (if it takes a minute, do it now), or the "one thing now" approach—choose one small gesture and follow through: a smile, a quick text, holding the door, starting the dishes because your partner is already juggling something heavy. Lower the bar from grand to doable, give yourself permission to be a little imperfect, and move. Each tiny follow-through rewrites your inner story from "I should" to "I do." The more often you cross the gap quickly, the smaller it becomes—until kindness isn't a plan, it's your reflex.

Intentionally making kindness and generosity a regular part of our lives takes consistent, small efforts. It's about weaving these acts into our everyday routines. Here are a few simple ways to cultivate a habit of generosity:

- Keep a stack of blank greeting cards handy and write a note whenever it crosses your mind.
- Compliment a stranger or thank them for their hard work.

109

- Offer your time by checking in on a friend, visiting a loved one, or volunteering.
- Pay for someone's coffee or meal and brighten their day.
- Share encouragement: text a friend, and remind them how amazing they are.
- Leave a positive review when you've had a good experience.
- Share your skills with someone. You could teach them a skill they'll have forever.
- Give up your seat to someone who may need it more, someone elderly or pregnant, perhaps.
- Donate your unwanted clothing or household items
- Leave a generous tip for great service.

Generosity doesn't have to be grand—it just has to be intentional. When we shift from thinking about kindness to acting on it, we strengthen our relationships, uplift others, and cultivate a life rich in joy, connection, and meaning.

One of the simplest, yet most impactful, acts of kindness costs nothing and takes only a second—making eye contact and offering a genuine smile. In a world where people are often lost in their phones, rushing from one place to the next, this small gesture can be incredibly meaningful. A smile acknowledges another person's presence, reminding them (and us) that we are seen, that we matter.

We never know what someone is going through; maybe they've had a hard day, are feeling lonely, or just need a small moment of warmth. A smile can be that moment. It doesn't require a conversation, just a brief exchange of positive energy.

A single smile can cause a contagious chain reaction, lifting spirits beyond what we can see.

So, the next time you cross paths with a stranger, resist the urge to look away or rush past. Instead, meet their eyes, offer a smile, and know that in that small moment, you've added a little more light to the world.

Setting an example of kindness can be as simple as someone witnessing our actions—sparking a new habit, fresh understanding, or ripple effect of their own. When my children were little, an elderly couple lived down the street from us. They had several mature oak trees, and their front yard was full of leaves. I drove past their house and thought about how difficult it would be for them to clean up their yard.

It was a sunshiny, crisp, fall day, and we had nothing planned. I instructed the three kids to grab gloves and rakes, and sneakers. We walked down the street and in no time had the neighbor's front yard clear of leaves. I hurried the kids along to finish the job before the neighbors returned home. "But they won't know we were the ones who raked their yard." one of my children said. I simply said, "That's ok. We will." Not all acts of kindness come with immediate feedback, or any feedback at all. Sometimes, you won't know the impact you had, but that doesn't mean it wasn't deeply felt.

Moments of connection often begin quietly, without fanfare. One Saturday summer morning, I sat on my front porch drinking my coffee in solitude while my teenagers slept in. I became aware of a tornado that had touched down and impacted a residential development in a town thirty minutes away. The images were devastating. Houses flattened; belongings strewn everywhere.

Everything in the tornado's path was destroyed. Families were misplaced, and pets were lost. The red cross was asking for volunteers to comb through the rubble for personal belongings. I woke up the kids, told them to get dressed, and we were out the door in minutes. We were not prepared for the shocking scene we came upon. Entire homes were reduced to tiny pieces of debris.

We were asked to look for anything that looked like a salvageable personal item. If we found a photo, we were to hold it up high and shout "photo," and someone would come to collect this cherished prize. I recently asked my children, now in their 30s and 40s, what impact that act of kindness had on them as teenagers. My daughter said, "It showed me how good it feels to do things for others".

Sometimes, we never know the impact of our kindness. Unconditional giving, especially when the recipient doesn't know who helped, shifts the focus entirely onto the *act* itself rather than the recognition. There's a special kind of joy that comes from knowing you helped someone simply because you could. That joy isn't tied to gratitude or applause; it's rooted in compassion, which creates a lasting inner peace.

We often think about kindness in terms of what we can do for others, but what about the moments when we are the ones on the receiving end? Take a moment to reflect. When was the last time someone surprised you with a random act of kindness? Maybe it was a stranger paying for your coffee, a friend sending you an unexpected note, or someone simply offering a few kind words when you needed them most.

How did it make you feel? Likely, it was more than just a nice moment; it may have shifted your entire day. Acts of kindness, no matter how small, remind us that we are connected, valued, and not alone. They reinforce the idea that goodness exists in the world, even in the most unexpected places.

When we remember how powerful kindness feels when received, it strengthens our desire to pass it on. A simple act of kindness can have a lasting impact, rippling far beyond what we can see. So, let's not just *think* about kindness when we can be the reason someone else feels that same warmth, encouragement or hope today. Let's close that gap between intention and action.

Questions to ponder:

1. Can you remember times when you didn't follow through on a random act of kindness you intended? How could you close the gap between intention and action?

2. When you were the recipient of generosity or kindness, how did it make you feel?

3. What actions can you implement to form a habit of generosity?

CHAPTER EIGHTEEN

Holding Myself Accountable
for My Wellness

In my role as a caregiver for my husband, I wandered through years of my life thinking I was taking care of myself. I had gradually reduced the importance of wellness to the most basic of things. I remember my dementia specialist scolding me, "Lisa, a bath is not self-care!" I really thought slipping away once a week for a bubble bath was enough.

After Peter died, I took a hard look at my daily habits. There were many areas that needed adjusting to bring me back to a place of well-being. I was depressed after experiencing such a devastating loss, and wine and Xanax had become my companions. I had given up my healthy habits of walking and working out, meditating, and eating to nourish my body instead of staving off hunger.

I realized that one of the keys to maintaining a healthy and balanced life is accountability. Not just to others, but to myself. Creating a system that works for me has been essential in sustaining my wellness journey. A daily point system helps me stay on track, not just physically but emotionally, mentally, and spiritually as well.

I created a spreadsheet to track the areas I want to focus on improving. Each time I meet a daily goal, I earn a point. If I don't complete the goal that day, no point. Simple as that.

My point system may shift week to week or month to month, depending on which goals need a little extra attention or motivation. This flexibility allows me to reward progress where it matters most—and give myself grace when something isn't a top priority.

I've set a weekly goal based on my tracking system, which breaks down into manageable, positive habits I can incorporate every day. These activities are ones that nourish my body, mind, and soul. Whether it's taking a walk, connecting with friends, or meditating for peace of mind, I've realized that these small actions compound into greater overall wellness.

I created my daily tracker out of a need for accountability and a deeper understanding of where I was truly spending my time and energy. It became clear to me that, despite having good intentions, I wasn't always meeting the goals I thought I was. I had to face the reality that I wasn't always following through with the self-care practices I valued so much. That's when I realized that without a system to track my progress, I was leaving too much to chance. The daily tracker became my way of keeping myself honest and intentional, offering a clear picture of my habits, while also helping me celebrate my successes and course-correct when needed. It's not about perfection, it's about creating consistent momentum, one small step at a time.

Motivation can come from different places, both within us and from the world around us. There's the internal drive, the kind that pushes us to do something because it aligns with what we truly value, things like growth, peace, or health. Then there's the external drive, like rewards or recognition, that comes from hitting milestones or seeing progress. For me, my motivation comes from both of these.

Each day, I aim to hit a set number of points across the following areas:

- Meditate: A few moments of stillness to center my thoughts.
- Games: Engaging my brain to stay alert and focused
- Work Out: Physical movement to keep my body strong and energized.
- Walk: My daily grounding practice that helps clear my mind.
- Service: A small act of kindness or volunteer work to stay connected to my community.
- Friends & Family: Cultivating relationships and nurturing connections.
- Water Consumption: Staying hydrated and keeping my energy up.
- Read: Feeding my mind with inspiration and knowledge.
- Weight Range: Staying mindful of my health goals.
- Vitamins: Taking care of my body with the right nutrition.
- Writing/Speaking: Focusing on my purpose, advocacy, and creative projects.

- Xanax: Eliminating the need for Xanax to sleep at night.
- Wine: Mindfully reducing alcohol intake for better overall health.
- Gratitude: A daily practice of acknowledging the good in my life.

Meditate: Taking time each day to meditate is like hitting the reset button for my mind. It allows me to center myself, clear out the mental clutter, and connect with my inner peace. Meditation helps me ground myself in the present moment, reducing stress and increasing clarity. Just a few minutes each morning can make a world of difference in how I approach the day. It's a reminder that peace isn't just something I find outside of me; it's something I create from within, intentionally.

Brain games: Online games like Wordle, crosswords, Sudoku, and logic puzzles are a simple, joyful way to keep your mind sharp and your mood lifted. They nudge multiple skills at once—attention, working memory, word retrieval, problem-solving, pattern recognition—and that mix helps build cognitive "reserve," the brain's capacity to adapt and stay resilient over time. You also get quick wins that release a little hit of motivation, lowering stress and boosting confidence (nothing like a finished grid to start the day). Best of all, it doesn't take much: five to ten minutes with your coffee, a puzzle while dinner is in the oven, or a Wordle shared with a friend for a spark of connection. Done consistently, these tiny practices add up—gentle daily reps that keep your brain curious, flexible, and engaged without demanding a huge block of time

Work Out: Movement is a non-negotiable for me. Whether it's strength training, yoga, or a full-on cardio session, working out gives me the energy and strength to take on anything. It's not just about physical health; it's a practice of self-respect. Each workout is a way of honoring my body, challenging myself, and feeling empowered. It keeps me strong, focused, and confident, and also has the bonus of boosting my mood through the release of endorphins. I've never regretted working out, but I have regretted not working out.

Walking: Walking might seem like a simple thing, but it's incredibly grounding for me. It's my chance to step outside, breathe in fresh air, and let my thoughts wander. Whether it's a quick walk or a longer hike, walking helps me stay connected to nature, refresh my mind, and improve my physical health. It's a practice of balance and a reminder that movement doesn't have to be intense to have a positive impact.

Service: Giving back is one of the most fulfilling things I do. Whether it's volunteering my time, offering a helping hand to a friend, or being present for a cause I care about, service nourishes my soul. It connects me to others and reminds me of the power of kindness and generosity. The act of serving is a way to contribute to something bigger than myself and reinforce the value of compassion in my life.

Friends & Family: Relationships are everything. The time I spend with my loved ones, whether it's a phone call, a shared meal, or quality time, is a vital part of my well-being. These connections give me support, love, and joy, and they remind me that I am never truly alone. Investing in relationships with family and friends nourishes my heart and helps me stay focused on what really matters.

Water Consumption: Staying hydrated is one of the simplest, yet most important ways to care for my body. Water is essential for every function in my system, and when I'm properly hydrated, I feel more energized, focused, and healthy. My skin and hair look their best when I'm meeting my hydration goal. It's easy to forget to drink enough water, but when I track it, I'm reminded to stay mindful and prioritize my body's needs.

Read: Reading is an important part of my personal growth. It expands my mind, fuels my creativity, and connects me to new ideas and perspectives. Whether it's for pleasure, learning, or self-improvement, reading gives me the chance to grow intellectually and emotionally. It's a way for me to stay curious and open to new possibilities, while also nurturing my own voice and thoughts.

Weight Range: Keeping track of my weight helps me stay aware of my physical health, but it's not just about the number on the scale. It's about maintaining balance and staying within a five-pound range that feels healthy and good for me. It's a gentle reminder to make choices that support my physical health, while also showing myself compassion in the process. It's not about perfection, it's about self-awareness and respecting my body. I feel healthiest and most confident when I stay in my weight range.

Vitamins: Taking vitamins is a way I support my overall health, ensuring that I'm getting the nutrients I need to feel my best. They help fill in any gaps that might exist in my diet and give me that extra support for energy, immunity, and wellness. It's a small but powerful act of self-care that shows I'm being proactive about my health.

Writing & Speaking: Writing about my experiences and reflections related to Alzheimer's and life in general is both therapeutic and meaningful. It helps me process my journey and share my insights with others. It keeps me connected to my mission and purpose, especially with my work in the Alzheimer's community. It's a way for me to offer support, raise awareness, and give a voice to those who no longer have one (through their caregivers), while also giving me a creative outlet for my emotions and ideas.

Xanax: I developed an unhealthy habit of relying on Xanax when I was depressed. While it felt like the perfect coping tool at the time, I needed to wean myself off and use other natural tools to lull myself to sleep. Incorporating relaxing strategies like a warm bath, reading, diffusing lavender, or putting my phone away earlier was a big help.

Wine: While enjoying a glass of wine can be a lovely way to unwind, tracking my consumption helps me stay mindful of how much I'm drinking. Moderation is key for me, and being aware of my habits helps me make healthier choices. It's not about eliminating wine completely but about finding balance and being in control of how I treat my body. It's easy for me to get off track and not realize how much wine I'm drinking. The daily tracker shows me in black and white when I need to rein it in!

Gratitude: Filling my day with gratitude is a practice that shifts my mindset to focus on what's going well, rather than what's not. It's easy to get caught up in the chaos of life, but taking time to reflect on the good things, big and small, helps me cultivate a positive outlook. Gratitude opens my heart and reminds me of the abundance that already exists in my life. It's the foundation of finding joy in every day.

There are days when I don't hit every goal, and that's okay. I've learned that wellness isn't about perfection; it's about the consistent effort to improve, even if progress looks

121

different day to day. I've learned to give myself grace when things don't go as planned. Life changes, and so do my priorities. Some weeks, I may be traveling, or there are new challenges with family or work. My goals adapt with the circumstances, and I focus on doing what I can in those moments. I no longer beat myself up if I miss a walk or if I don't hit my weight range. What matters is that I remain compassionate with myself and get back on track when I can.

Each of these practices isn't just a checkbox to tick off; it's a way of aligning my daily actions with my deeper values. They serve as a constant reminder of what truly matters to me: my physical health, emotional well-being, and the relationships I hold dear. When I make time for meditation, movement, hydration, or reading, I'm not just completing a task; I'm creating space for growth, healing, and connection. These practices ground me in the present, help me stay centered amidst the chaos, and empower me to show up for myself in the most authentic way possible. And when I show up for myself, I'm better equipped to show up for others, with more energy, patience, and love to give. It's about cultivating balance, because when I'm in balance, I can truly live with intention and be the best version of myself.

Questions to ponder:

1. Are there goals you'd like to hold yourself accountable for?

2. What motivates you to stay on track?

3. Can you treat yourself with grace and kindness when you don't meet your goal?

CHAPTER NINETEEN

Choosing Curiosity Over Judgment

One of the greatest shifts we can make on our journey toward peace and self-compassion is replacing judgment with curiosity. Judgment is sharp and final; it boxes us into rigid conclusions about ourselves, others, and the world. Curiosity, on the other hand, is open and expansive. It invites us to ask questions, to explore, and to see challenges and missteps not as proof of failure, but as invitations to learn and grow.

When we slip into judgment, it often sounds like: "I should have known better." "I'm not good enough." "They're wrong. I'm right." Judgment locks us into fixed thinking and robs us of the opportunity to understand more deeply. But when we choose curiosity instead, we soften. We might ask, "Why did I react that way?" "What might they have been feeling?" "What can I learn from this moment?" This small but powerful shift changes everything. It moves us from a posture of defense to one of discovery.

Curiosity reminds us that we are not static beings; we're constantly evolving. Every mistake, every uncomfortable feeling, every unexpected twist in the path is simply information. It's data, not a verdict. Through curiosity, we develop a more compassionate relationship with ourselves. Instead of demanding perfection, we marvel at our growth. Instead of berating ourselves for feeling anxious, angry, or uncertain, we wonder, "What is this feeling trying to tell me?"

I remember hearing a story about a man and his four small children on a train. The man sat quietly while his children acted rambunctiously, climbing on the seats and boisterously laughing and playing with each other. Some would judge their behavior as ill-mannered and rude. Why was the father not reprimanding his children? He seemed oblivious to how disruptive they were behaving.

Finally, a passenger who was at her wits' end, commented to the father about his children. The man responded, "I'm sorry. We just buried their mother. It's the first time I've heard them laugh and play in more than a week. I don't have the heart to stop them."

This story has stayed with me because it's such a powerful reminder that we never see the full picture of someone else's life. What looks like carelessness or disrespect might actually be grief, survival, or a quiet act of love. Curiosity over judgment invites us to soften our assumptions and open our hearts to possibilities beyond what we immediately see. When we choose to lean into understanding instead of frustration, we create space for compassion, not just for others, but for ourselves too.

In relationships, choosing curiosity over judgment can transform conflict into connection. Rather than assuming bad intent, we can get curious about someone else's experience. Instead of deciding how things *should* be, we can lean into *what is*, with openness and a willingness to understand. Curiosity doesn't mean we excuse harmful behavior; it means we seek deeper truth before rushing to conclusions.

Ultimately, curiosity is an act of love. It honors our complexities. It makes room for our humanity and authenticity. And it creates space for a gentler, wiser way of moving through the world; one rooted not in fear or criticism, but in wonder, compassion, and growth.

Judging others often happens so quickly that we don't even realize it. A snap opinion about someone's actions, choices, or even their appearance can flash through our minds before we've had a chance to pause. But judgment, whether silent or spoken, creates separation. It builds walls between us and others based on assumptions rather than understanding. When we judge a situation or a person, we place ourselves in a position of perceived superiority, distancing ourselves from shared human experience.

The first step toward shifting from judgment to curiosity is simply noticing. Judgment tends to come with a few telltale emotional signatures: tightness in the chest, irritation, impatience, or a sense of superiority or moral high ground. When we feel that tightening, that "they're wrong" or "this shouldn't be happening" energy rise within us, it's a signal, a gentle tap on the shoulder, to pause.

When we catch ourselves judging, we can ask reflective questions:

- "What story am I telling myself about this person or situation?"
- "Do I have all the information?"
- "What else could be true here?"

Even just recognizing the moment of judgment is a huge win. Awareness is the doorway to transformation. Once we notice judgment bubbling up, the next step is to soften it with curiosity. Curiosity sounds like wonder. It sounds like compassion. It invites open-ended exploration rather than firm conclusions.

Here's a simple practice: when you catch yourself judging, silently replace the judgment with a question. Instead of, "That's ridiculous," you might wonder, "What led them to see it that way?" Instead of, "I would never do that," you might ask, "What experiences have shaped their choices?" Over time, this practice becomes second nature. It rewires the way we interpret the world, infusing it with more patience, understanding, and grace.

Forming a habit of curiosity over judgment starts with a small but powerful shift: noticing. It's not about never having judgmental thoughts (we're human, after all!), but about catching ourselves in the act with kindness. The moment you realize you're making a snap judgment—about a friend who's late, a stranger who's short with you, or even yourself—you can pause and get curious instead.

At first, it might feel awkward or forced, but the more we practice, the more natural it becomes. It's like building a muscle. Each time you choose curiosity, you're teaching your mind to widen its lens instead of narrowing it. You create a gap between the moment something happens and the story you tell yourself about it—and in that gap, there's room for grace, understanding, and even connection.

Another way to reinforce the habit is to stay playful with it. Turn it into a little game: when you catch yourself judging, give yourself a point if you can think of three alternative explanations. Over time, you'll find that curiosity becomes your first instinct rather than judgment, and life feels a whole lot lighter when you stop carrying the weight of assumptions around with you.

Once we've developed the muscle of choosing curiosity over judgment in our own lives, we naturally want to share this liberating perspective with others. But it's important to remember that pushing people to change often feels like judgment in disguise. The goal isn't to correct or "fix" someone's mindset; it's to model curiosity in the way we interact.

You might invite curiosity in others by asking gentle, open-ended questions like:

- "I wonder why that might be?"
- "Have you ever thought about it this way?"
- "What do you think their perspective could be?"

Share your own process, not as advice, but as personal insight: "I used to jump to conclusions too, but lately I've been trying to ask myself what else might be going on. It's really helped me feel less stressed." When we lead with vulnerability and non-judgment, others feel safe to consider a different way of seeing, without feeling criticized or wrong.

Ultimately, encouraging curiosity in others starts with embodying it ourselves, through our tone, our energy, and our genuine compassion. As always, the way we live becomes our greatest teacher.

You're at the grocery store, and the cashier is short with you, no smile, no chit-chat. It's easy to think, "How rude!" But curiosity invites a different thought: "Maybe they're having a really hard day. Maybe they just got bad news, or they're overwhelmed." That small shift not only softens your experience but allows you to meet the moment with kindness instead of resentment. Curiosity dissolves these walls. Curiosity invites empathy. It reminds us that everyone is doing the best they can with the tools, awareness, and experiences they have in the moment. Just like we are.

Instead of instantly labeling the cashier as rude or unfriendly, we can pause and choose to stay open. We can reframe the judgment by wondering what they may be carrying that we can't see.

I recall an instance when my next-door neighbor was having a large tree cut down on the common edge of our properties. I had planted a new perennial garden a few feet from the tree. The tree company dropped large branches on the garden and walked over the plants all afternoon. When I realized what had happened, I stormed outside and insisted the foreman bring his bucket down to the ground so I could give him a piece of my mind.

Looking back, that feels a bit embarrassing now, but the stress of caregiving had my emotions unraveled. There were certainly other ways I could have handled the situation. I should have waited until the job was finished and addressed it with less emotion. I'm sure I was judged harshly, rather than met with empathy and understanding.

You don't have to excuse bad behavior, but when you allow space for the unknown, you protect your own peace. You might even smile warmly and say something simple like, "I hope the rest of your day is gentle on you." Sometimes, a little kindness can break the ice, and even if it doesn't, you walk away lighter, having chosen compassion over assumption. The goal isn't to fix them, it's to choose the energy you want to carry forward.

You can't be curious and harsh at the same time. True curiosity is infused with compassion. When we choose to wonder about someone's unseen struggles, motivations, or wounds, we naturally become softer, and our world becomes a more gracious place to live in.

When we approach the world through the lens of curiosity, we are essentially saying, "I want to understand." Compassion takes it one step further and says, "I want to understand so that I can meet this person (or myself) with kindness, not criticism." Curiosity without compassion can sometimes veer into judgment disguised as interest. We might be curious in a way that still labels, separates, or subtly blames. True compassion transforms curiosity into something healing, a tool for connection rather than control.

When we're curious *with compassion*, we aren't just gathering facts or trying to fix or figure someone out. We are leaning into the truth that every person (including ourselves) carries unseen battles, hidden hurts, and complex layers of humanity.

Compassionate curiosity builds empathy, which builds connection, which builds trust. It's a ripple effect, and it starts the moment we pause and choose wonder over assumption, grace over judgment.

Questions to ponder:

1. How can we gently guide a conversation back to curiosity when a group starts slipping into judgment?

2. When you notice yourself judging, how can you pause and reframe your thoughts with compassion?

3. How might your relationships change if you approached misunderstandings with curiosity instead of criticism?

CHAPTER TWENTY

Healing Through Helping

There's something profoundly sacred about giving back, especially when your heart has been shattered and reshaped by grief. For me, giving back hasn't just been about helping others; it's been a lifeline. A tether to purpose. A balm to the parts of me that ached after losing Peter. And over time, it's become a meaningful part of how I continue to love him, even now.

When Peter and I were navigating the relentless path of early-onset Alzheimer's, I promised myself that when the time came, I would use everything we endured, every lesson, every strategy, every raw moment, to support others. It was one way I could honor our love story. One way I could turn pain into purpose.

Peter and I had an unspoken agreement that his life and legacy would matter in a way we couldn't understand then. Peter gave me a beautiful life, but he gave the world a beautiful gift: the gift of his permission to share his story openly and transparently. My promise to Peter was that I would be his voice, sharing our truths while protecting his dignity.

That promise has blossomed into something I never could have fully imagined in those early days of caregiving. Today, I find healing and strength in the ways I show up for others. I advocate to legislators, bridging the gap between policy and personal experience. I like to call it the conduit between congressmen and caregivers. When I speak with lawmakers, I bring Peter with me, not in body, but in story, in legacy. I talk about what it means to care for someone with Alzheimer's. I highlight the sacrifices caregivers make, the emotional and financial toll, and the urgent need for support. These conversations don't always lead to immediate change, but they plant seeds. They humanize the data. They make a difference.

Writing our story in *Oh Hello, Alzheimer's* was another act of advocacy, and one of the most vulnerable things I've ever done. I shared our journey intimately: the moments of confusion, heartbreak, laughter, and love. The ways we preserved joy in the face of decline. The strategies I discovered to reduce stress and create calm. I wrote not as an expert, but as a wife, a witness, and a woman who didn't want anyone else to feel as alone as I sometimes did.

What I didn't expect was how many people would reach out afterward, caregivers from all over, telling me that my words helped them feel seen. That they cried reading about Peter because they saw their own spouse, parent, or friend in him. That they learned something practical, they could use the very next day. There is no greater honor than hearing that your pain has created comfort for someone else.

In the months and years after Peter's passing, I also began offering private virtual consultations to caregivers. Sometimes they needed help sorting through resources or planning next steps. Other times, they just needed someone to listen who truly understood. These calls reminded me of the power of connection and how just a few grounded, compassionate words can shift someone's entire day. I've stepped back from doing them regularly, but I still cherish the impact of those conversations and the mutual healing they brought.

I also began speaking at memory care facilities, sharing our story and advocating for compassionate caregiving. These talks aren't always easy, but they're deeply fulfilling. I meet families who are desperate for hope, validation, and guidance. I meet staff who want to do right by their residents but feel overwhelmed or undertrained. Through storytelling, I try to paint a picture of what it looks like to step into someone's reality, to preserve dignity, to say yes to connection even when words fade.

Most recently, I was invited to be the keynote speaker at the annual conference of the Virginia Coalition for the Prevention of Elder Abuse. Standing in front of a room full of professionals, social workers, attorneys, caregivers, and EMTs, I felt both the weight and the beauty of shared responsibility. I spoke about compassionate caregiving and radical acceptance, about the difference it makes when we meet people where they are. The feedback I received afterward was humbling. People told me they felt recharged, inspired, less alone. And I realized again that giving back isn't just something I do for others, it's something that keeps my heart soft and open.

Fundraising has also been a powerful part of this journey. I lead a team each year for the Walk to End Alzheimer's, and together we've raised over $90,000. The walk is more than a fundraiser, it's a sacred gathering. A field of people united by love and loss, all walking with purpose. Each name on a t-shirt, each flower in a hand, tells a story. And with every step, we declare: this matters. These lives matter. The fight for better treatment—for better care, for a cure matters.

This year, I accepted the invitation to be the 2025 Executive Chair of the Greater Hartford Walk to End Alzheimer's. It's an honor and a responsibility I hold with gratitude. It means mentoring new team captains, recruiting volunteers, connecting with sponsors, and continuing to build awareness. It means showing up as a leader for something bigger than myself. I'm also a board member of the Connecticut Chapter of the Alzheimer's Association, a role that allows me to help shape the direction of programs and support services for families in our state. It's a seat at the table that I hold in honor of Peter, and for every family still in the thick of the journey.

Even though I've chosen a grand, more public way to serve, this may not be for everyone. Sometimes it's a phone call, text, handwritten note, or a moment of listening. Sometimes it's sharing your story, even when your voice trembles or emotions take over. Sometimes it's simply choosing to keep your heart open when it would be easier to shut down.

Giving back has helped me heal. It reminds me that I am not just someone who lost, I am someone who loves. Who continues to love. And who believes that the most powerful way to honor someone you've lost is to keep reaching for joy, connection, and impact. Peter would want that.

I'll never stop missing Peter. But I'll also never stop carrying him forward. And every time someone tells me that hearing our story helped them feel less alone, I know I've done just that. Giving back is a quiet kind of legacy. It's how we say: love didn't end here. It lives on in the choices we make, the people we lift, and the hope we pass on. That, to me, has been healing through helping.

Moving forward, I reflect on a time when giving back felt like the only thing keeping me grounded. In the wake of Peter's death, I needed somewhere to place the love that had nowhere to go. Volunteering with the Alzheimer's Association became that place. It allowed me to channel my grief into something meaningful, not just for myself, but for others walking their own difficult paths. In giving, I found healing. In showing up, I found pieces of myself again.

This chapter of giving has been one of the most fulfilling of my life. It allowed me to keep Peter close while also reaching forward. But lately, I've felt a quiet shift, an invitation to grow in new ways. Not because the work no longer matters, but because I am evolving. What once felt like everything now feels like one meaningful thread in a much larger tapestry. I'm learning that making space for what's next doesn't diminish what's come before. It honors it.

As I look ahead, I know I'll be stepping back from some of the responsibilities I've held within the Alzheimer's Association. That decision didn't come quickly, and it doesn't come without emotion. But it comes from a place of peace, of listening to the still, wise voice within me that says it's time to follow new curiosities, deepen other parts of myself, and explore fresh ways of connecting, giving and loving. It's not a goodbye. It's a gentle shift.

I will carry this chapter of my life with me always. The lessons, the people, the Wal to End Alzheimer's, the quiet moments of shared understanding, they've shaped me. They've reminded me that giving back isn't just about the cause. It's about who we become when we open our hearts. Wherever this next chapter leads, I know it will still be rooted in service, purpose, and love. Just with new colors, new rhythms, and new ways of finding joy.

Questions to ponder:

1. In what ways have you experienced healing through helping others?

2. Is there a part of your life that you feel called to give more?

3. Are you saying yes to anything that no longer feels aligned?

CHAPTER TWENTY-ONE

No Regrets, Only Lessons

In previous chapters, we explored forgiveness and acceptance as being essential when it comes to navigating regret. Regret is a complex emotion we feel when we believe we've done something wrong, or failed to act when we should have. It often shows up as sadness, disappointment, or guilt over a past event or missed opportunity. The first step in understanding regret is to examine the emotion itself. It usually stems from decisions made—or not made—and the perceived consequences that followed.

Regret can sound like a whisper: *"Why didn't I do that differently?"* or *"What if I had only known then what I know now?"* It carries the weight of hindsight, offering us a view of the past colored by the clarity we didn't have at the time. And in that way, regret is almost always unfair. It asks us to judge our old selves with the wisdom of our present selves.

One night, I was driving home from a gathering with friends, and I was reflecting on conversations I had had. One gave me an uneasy feeling of regret. I had yammered on excitedly about the things going on in my life, but had not asked many questions about what was happening in hers. I regretted it immediately. I felt ashamed, selfish, and embarrassed, and I felt guilty for not reciprocating her interest.

I decided to text her when I got home. "I don't feel like we had enough time together. I want to hear all about what's happening with your new business and your family. Would you have time for lunch or dinner next week? We need some quiet quality time together."

Rather than grazing on my shame and guilt, I chose to learn a lesson. Be interesting and interested. When I focus on asking more questions than I answer in a conversation, I become a better friend. I learn things about people that I didn't know, and relationships have grown deeper because of it. Ironically, that friend now frequently comments, "Thank you for always being so interested in my life." What a powerful lesson!

I'm well aware that my text is riddled with justification for my actions. "I don't feel like we had enough time together," created an excuse for my behavior. There was plenty of time, I just didn't use it in a way that honored my values. My plan was once we were together at lunch, I could be more honest and forthcoming, "I realized I answered a lot of your questions, but didn't ask you about what's going on. I didn't make the effort I should have, so I wanted to correct that right away." In handling the situation this way, I made my friend feel valued and deepened our connection.

That experience reminded me of a simple truth: at its core, regret is tied to love, hope, and meaning. We only regret the things that mattered deeply to us. We don't carry the same ache for every misstep. It's the choices involving our values, our relationships, and our own integrity that linger. Regret often signals a disconnect between who we were and who we want to be. It arises from missed opportunities, unmet expectations, or actions that didn't align with our inner truth.

But here's the thing: regret doesn't have to be a prison. It can be a portal—a doorway into deeper understanding. When we lean into it, not to wallow or shame ourselves, but to listen, it can teach us. It reveals what we value most, and sometimes it hands us the map back to ourselves. Regret doesn't have to mean failure. It can mean we've grown. It means we now know better, and with that knowing comes the power to do better moving forward, culminating in beautiful self-growth.

We replace guilt with self-compassion through forgiveness, reminding ourselves that we were doing the best we could with what we knew at the time. None of us is perfect. We're all learning, often in real time and under pressure. If we can meet our regrets with compassion, we can turn them into something beautiful: not weights to carry, but lessons to live by.

The emotions that come with regret—guilt—shame, sadness—can be consuming if we let them take root without tending to them. But the beautiful thing about emotions is that they're not fixed; they're fluid. They can shift when we become intentional about how we respond to them. When regret shows up, instead of pushing it away or getting stuck in the "should haves," we can get curious. What is this feeling trying to teach me? That simple question opens the door to transformation.

We replace shame with acceptance, gently acknowledging our humanity and all its beautiful imperfections. Sadness softens when we invite in gratitude. Not necessarily for the regret itself, but for the clarity it gave us and the way it reshaped our intentions.

Radical acceptance is the quiet, courageous act of meeting reality exactly as it is, without judgment, resistance, or the endless loop of "should have." It doesn't mean we approve of

141

everything that's happened, or that we wouldn't have chosen differently. It simply means we stop fighting with the past. We acknowledge the moment, the choice, the outcome. Not to give up, but to free ourselves from the emotional weight of wishing it were something else.

Joy, peace, and fulfillment don't come from pretending regret doesn't exist; they come from using regret as a stepping stone. In that way, we reclaim the narrative. We get to say, "This moment taught me something valuable. And because of it, I'm choosing differently now." That healing is so impactful!

Another powerful shift is to replace rumination with purpose. If something you regret still tugs at your heart, ask how it can fuel you forward. Could it make you more empathetic? More intentional in how you love or lead or listen? When we turn our attention to how we can grow from the experience, the emotional weight lightens. We begin to carry wisdom instead of a burden.

With that wisdom, we shift our focus from *what went wrong* to *what we've learned*, and we invite in a softer kind of strength. The moment we ask, "How did I experience growth through this regret?" or "What clarity did this experience bring?" we begin to unburden ourselves. The pain doesn't vanish, but it transforms. It becomes a teacher, not a tormentor.

And with that transformation comes wisdom, earned, embodied, and deeply personal. That wisdom isn't just for us. It becomes something we can offer the world.

- We can teach empathy because we've felt misunderstood.
- We can teach self-forgiveness because we've walked through shame and found light on the other side.

142

- We can teach resilience, not because we were never knocked down, but because we stood back up. Wiser, kinder, more whole.

We teach by living the lessons out loud. By sharing our stories with vulnerability. By creating space for others to feel less alone in theirs. And maybe most of all, we teach by modeling what it looks like to grow from our regrets instead of shrinking because of them.

Questions to ponder:

1. What is one regret you carry that still feels heavy, and why?

2. What did this experience teach you, and how have you grown because of it?

3. How might you use this experience to help someone else?

CHAPTER TWENTY-TWO

Listening to My Intuition, My Internal Guidance System

We're often taught to prize logic, strategy, and external validation as our guides. But some of the most important decisions in my life, especially the ones that led to peace, didn't come from spreadsheets or external consensus. They came from something quieter and deeper: my intuition, supported by my emotions.

Intuition and emotion are often dismissed as "soft" or even unreliable. But what I've learned is this: when I tune in to that inner voice and truly listen to what I'm feeling, I find a clarity no outside expert can give me. This isn't just poetic or spiritual, it's practical. My intuition is the compass that never steers me wrong when I'm brave enough to follow it. And my emotions? They're not random or messy, they're messengers, gently (and sometimes loudly) showing me where something is off or deeply right.

In a world that moves fast and praises certainty, learning to trust your gut can feel radical. But the more I've leaned into this way of navigating life, the more peace I've found. Not because everything goes perfectly, but because I'm no longer in constant conflict with myself. In this chapter, I want to show you how to recognize, trust, and strengthen your own internal compass, because it's already there, waiting for you to listen.

Intuition is often described as a "gut feeling," a sense of knowing that shows up before logic has time to explain it. It's subtle, yet powerful, a quiet whisper rather than a shout. It's the feeling you get when something just feels off, even if everything looks fine on paper. Or the deep sense of *yes* that rises in your chest when you're heading in the right direction, even if it doesn't make sense to anyone else.

Unlike fear, which is loud, urgent, and demanding, intuition tends to feel calm, even if it's nudging you toward a big change. It's steady and grounded. It doesn't pressure you, it invites you. And it often shows up in the body: a flutter in the chest, a pit in the stomach, a sense of expansion or contraction.

Our emotions are part of this same inner guidance system. They aren't problems to fix, they're information and communication. Sadness might be telling you something needs to be released. Anger might signal a boundary that's been crossed. And joy? That's a flashing green light that says, more of this, please! When we learn to listen without judgment, we begin to see emotions not as interruptions, but as incredibly wise and personal messengers.

Intuition and emotion, when honored together, create a powerful inner compass, one that can guide you toward alignment, authenticity, and peace. The key is learning to recognize their voices and trust that they're speaking for your highest good.

For anyone who's ever been told that intuition is just woo-woo nonsense or airy-fairy emotional fluff, this part is for you.

There's actually real science behind those gut feelings and emotional nudges we get. Our gut has often been called the "second brain," and it's not just a catchy phrase. It holds over 100 million neurons and is constantly communicating with our brain through something called the gut-brain axis. Dr. Michael Gershon, who literally wrote the book on this, *The Second Brain*, found that the gut does a lot more than digest. It *thinks*, it processes, it knows. That flip in your stomach when something feels off? It's not just nerves. It's your inner wisdom waving a flag before your brain catches up.

And when it comes to intuition, we're not just guessing. Psychologist Gary Klein studied people who had to make split-second decisions—firefighters—ER doctors—soldiers and he found they weren't flying blind. They were recognizing patterns their brains had stored through years of experience. That quiet "knowing" comes from deep within, and it's often more reliable than a long list of pros and cons.

Then there's emotional intelligence, something Daniel Goleman brought to the surface in a big way. His research showed that the people who thrive, both personally and professionally, are the ones who tune into their emotions. Emotions aren't something to power through or ignore; they're information. They help us understand where we are, what we need, and what matters most to us as individuals.

And if you're more of a heart-led thinker, the HeartMath Institute has done some fascinating work showing how our emotional states and heart rhythms affect clarity, creativity, and yes, even intuition. When we're emotionally grounded, we can actually access deeper insights with more ease.

So yes, there's science. But let's not forget the soul. Because underneath all the neurons and research is something you already know: that soft pull inside, the sense of peace or discomfort that rises before you've even found the words. Whether you call it your gut, your spirit, your higher self, or just your inner knowing, it's your intuition. Many spiritual traditions recognize this as divine guidance. In Christianity, it might be the 'still, small voice' of God. In Buddhism, it's mindfulness, attuning you to the present. Across faiths, this inner wisdom is honored as a sacred compass. And it's worth listening to. When we trust it, we live in alignment instead of anxiety.

So, how do you actually know when your intuition is speaking? Start with how you feel. Your emotions are like a personalized internal GPS, always sending signals, always guiding. When something lights you up, when you feel a flutter of excitement, curiosity, or even calm clarity, that's your inner wisdom saying, *yes, this way*. You'll feel more energized, more open, more in flow. You'll sense alignment. It might not be logical. It might not even make sense to anyone else. But it feels *right*. That feeling? It's gold.

On the flip side, when something drains you, makes you feel tight, tense, or uneasy, it's a signal to pause. That doesn't mean you're doing something "wrong," it just means something's off, and it's time to gently re-align. These negative feelings aren't failures; they're feedback. Author and speaker Esther Hicks, known for her work on the Law of Attraction, puts it beautifully: *"You always know how well you're doing by how you feel. The better you feel, the more you are in alignment with who you really are."* That's the compass. Follow what feels better.

Your intuition often whispers instead of shouts. It shows up as a quiet knowing, a gut nudge, a phrase you can't shake, or a dream that keeps tapping your shoulder. Sometimes it looks like excitement. Sometimes it's simply a sense of peace when you think about taking a particular step.

The more you practice tuning in to how things feel and honoring those feelings, the clearer it gets. Like any relationship, your connection with your intuition deepens when you listen, trust, and act on what it tells you.

Start asking:

- What makes you feel open and motivated?
- What feels heavy?
- What gives me energy, and what drains it?
- What do I feel pulled toward, even if I can't explain why?

Let those feelings guide your next small step. Because when you follow what lights you up, you're walking the path that was always meant for you.

Trusting your intuition isn't a one-time decision; it's a practice. The more you use it, the stronger and clearer it becomes. Like a muscle, it grows through attention and repetition. One of the simplest ways to strengthen it is to create quiet. Not necessarily silence, but stillness. When you're always busy, always doing, always distracted, it's harder to hear your inner voice. But when you slow down, even just for a few minutes, that inner wisdom starts to come through. It might sound like a clear thought, or feel like a gentle nudge, or even appear as an image or memory. Give it space. Breathe. Ask yourself: *What does my soul need to know right now?* Then listen, without rushing to answer.

Journaling is another powerful tool. Write without filtering. Ask a question and let your pen move. You might be surprised by what comes out. Some people call it intuitive writing or soul scribbling. I just call it getting out of your own way. Often, we already know what's true, we just haven't slowed down enough to hear it.

Pay attention to patterns. If the same message keeps showing up, through conversations, songs, dreams, or random coincidences, don't dismiss it. That's your intuition waving at you through life's little synchronicities. The universe has a way of repeating itself when it really wants you to listen.

And most importantly, notice how you feel after you act on your intuition. Did things flow more easily? Did you feel lighter, more at peace, even if the outcome wasn't exactly what you expected? That's a sign you're on the right track. Let those moments build your trust.

Strengthening your intuition is not about being perfect or right all the time. It's about creating a relationship with yourself that's built on curiosity, compassion, and honesty. It's about tuning in, not checking out. It's about letting your inner guidance lead with grace.

While recognizing and strengthening your intuition is key, allowing life to flow without an exhaustive grip is where the real magic happens. However, allowing isn't passive; it's an active, intentional act of surrender. It's about letting go of the need to micromanage every detail, to control the outcome, or to make things happen on your own timeline.

When we talk about intuition and emotional guidance, allowing is the piece that creates the flow. It's trusting that you don't have to know everything right now. You don't have to have all the answers, nor do you need to know how every step will unfold. This is where trust comes in. Trust in your ability to recognize your intuition and confidence that the universe, or whatever higher power you believe in, will provide the next step when you're ready.

Allowing is where we give ourselves permission to listen to that quiet voice, to follow the guidance, and then step back and let things reveal themselves in their own time. When you allow life to flow rather than forcing it, you create space for more peace, more ease, and more synchronicity. And it's here where you start to see the results of your intuition in action.

Allowing isn't about being passive. It's about softening. It's about releasing the grip on how things should go and trusting that your intuition, paired with your willingness to let go, will guide you where you need to be. Another one of my favorite Esther Hicks quotes is: *"When you're in the process of allowing, you are allowing your natural state of well-being to flow."* And in that flow, peace is not only possible, it's inevitable.

When we trust our intuition and allow ourselves to follow its guidance, we begin to experience the *real* evidence of its power: peace. Peace isn't just the absence of noise or conflict; it's a deep, unwavering sense of rightness that flows from within, no matter the external circumstances. It's the calm that settles over us when we make a decision that's aligned with our inner wisdom, even if it doesn't make sense on the surface.

The more you lean into this, the more you'll realize that peace is the ultimate proof. Peace becomes the foundation upon which everything else rests. It's the quiet assurance that you're exactly where you need to be.

Questions to ponder:

1. Are there any areas in your life where you're feeling "off"? How can you start to realign with your intuition to bring more peace into those situations?

2. What does peace feel like for you? Can you recall a moment when peace settled over you, even in uncertainty? What was happening in that moment?

3. Are you anticipating any change that stirs a feeling of excitement? What lights you up?

CHAPTER TWENTY-THREE

Spirituality and Trust in the Universe

I grew up surrounded by the traditions of the Brethren faith, later marrying into a Jewish family. Through these experiences, I developed a deep respect for all expressions of belief, but if I'm being honest, none of them ever felt like they fully fit the shape of my soul.

It wasn't until I began exploring spirituality, not as a set of rigid rules, but as a personal and evolving connection, that something finally clicked. Spirituality wasn't about worshiping an external force; it was about honoring my higher self, cultivating gratitude, offering service, and continuously seeking growth with grace and compassion. It felt natural, peaceful, like coming home to something I had always known deep down. In spirituality, I found not just answers, but a deeper way of living. One grounded in trust, curiosity, and the gentle unfolding of who I am meant to be.

Now, I know some people hear words like "manifestation" and "trust the universe" and immediately roll their eyes, thinking it's all a little too "airy-fairy" or "woo-woo." And honestly? I get it. I used to feel that way, too. But what I've realized is that spirituality isn't about floating away from reality;

it's about being *more* grounded in it. It's not about pretending life is always perfect or magical. It's about believing that even in the hard moments, something good can grow. It's about paying attention to the energy you're putting into the world and trusting that it matters. You don't have to be burning sage under the full moon (unless you want to!) to believe that your thoughts, choices, and energy are shaping your life every day. It's really less "airy" and more about being *intentional*, and that's something that feels pretty practical once you start living it.

There's a certain magic that comes when we stop trying to control everything and instead trust in the flow of life. Over time, I have defined trusting in the flow of life as knowing that the Universe is always conspiring in my favor, even when I can't see the full picture yet. Spirituality, for me, isn't a set of rules. It's a way of *being* in the world: open, curious, trusting. This chapter is about all the ways I've learned to align with that energy and the daily practices that help me stay connected to something bigger than myself.

One of the biggest shifts I've made on this journey is learning to attract instead of chase. Chasing feels frantic, like you're grasping for something just out of reach. It's exhausting and, honestly, it usually pushes the very thing you want even further away. Attracting, though, feels calm and rooted. It's trusting that what's meant for me will find me, without me having to force or hustle for it.

When I stopped chasing friendships that felt one-sided and just focused on being the kind of friend I wanted to have, the right people started showing up. When I stopped stressing over opportunities and simply poured my heart into doing what I loved, doors opened without me banging them down. Attracting is about standing in your own light and letting the right things come to you naturally. It's a practice of trust. In yourself, in the timing, and in the universe: the bigger picture, that's always working in your favor.

The Law of Attraction teaches us that like attracts like. The energy we put out into the world—our thoughts—beliefs—emotions—acts like a magnet, draws in experiences that match that frequency. Conversely, when we focus on what's missing, we tend to attract more lack. But when we shift our attention to gratitude, joy, and possibility, life begins to reflect those things back to us. This isn't about pretending everything is perfect or forcing positive thoughts. It's about gently tuning into the feeling of what we want to experience, even before it shows up.

I've learned that the most powerful way to work with the Law of Attraction isn't through effortful wishing or chasing, it's through alignment. Becoming the version of myself who already feels peaceful, already feels loved, already trusts that good things are unfolding. It's not about controlling every outcome. It's about embodying the energy of trust and allowing life to meet me there.

This practice, of thinking, feeling, and acting from a place of worthiness, has shifted so much in my life. When I lead with that quiet confidence, when I speak with kindness, move through the world with gratitude, and believe in the possibility of good things, I start to notice more of them. It's as though the universe whispers back, "Yes, more of this." And when those moments arrive, the ones that fall into place with ease and feel almost too good to be true, I smile and say what I always do: *"Everything is always working out for me!"*

If the Law of Attraction is about energy, the Law of Assumption is about belief. It's the idea that what we assume to be true becomes true for us. When I assume that good things are always working out for me, that the universe is always supporting me, I start to notice evidence of that truth everywhere. This law invites me to act from the assumption that my dreams are already unfolding, rather than waiting for proof. It's a deep internal shift, from doubt to certainty, from hoping to knowing.

The Law of Assumption encourages us to move through the world with a subtle posture of *"of course."* Of course, I'm supported. Of course, I'm loved. Of course, things are lining up. It's not about arrogance, it's about alignment. It's the quiet confidence that flows from believing in the reality of something before it's visible.

Instead of passively waiting for life to show me a sign, I begin to live as if the sign has already arrived. I start behaving, choosing, and speaking as the version of me who already trusts. And as I do, my outer life gradually begins to match that inner knowing.

This doesn't mean we never waver. Doubt still shows up sometimes. But with the Law of Assumption, the key isn't perfection, it's practice. Every time I return to the mindset of *"of course,"* I'm strengthening that belief and reorienting my experience.

What we assume becomes a lens. And when we shift the lens to possibility, grace, and worthiness, we begin to see the world in those colors. It's not magic, it's a way of being that gradually magnetizes the life we were always meant to live.

Assumption and knowing lead us to allowance. One of the most powerful things I've learned is that allowance is not weakness, it's strength. Allowing means giving space for life to move, without clinging to how it "should" look. Letting go isn't giving up, it's releasing attachment to the outcome and trusting that something even better may be in motion. It's been humbling (and healing) to realize that my plans are often just a tiny glimpse of what's actually possible. By loosening my grip, I make room for the universe to work its magic in ways I could never have scripted.

At the core of this journey is trust, the kind of trust that isn't always logical but is deeply felt. Trusting the universe means believing that even when things don't make sense, they are unfolding perfectly. It's trusting that delays are redirections, not denials. Those obstacles are opportunities to grow. Trust isn't passive. It's an active choice to lean into faith rather than fear, over and over again. It's believing, even on the days when there's no visible reason to, that something beautiful is already on its way.

After Peter died, and the dark depression lifted, I was left with a trust that my experience with intense grief was a part of my story, not my entire story. I knew there was more to come. I believed wholeheartedly that after experiencing such a devastating tragedy, the Universe would surely take care of me and offer me grace.

In so many circumstances, large and small, when I expect something good to come, something even better shows up. Whether it's a front row parking space, a positive outcome of a difficult conversation, or a life partner, the more I trust and believe, the more the Universe continues to surprise me.

As a widow, I expected that Peter was the only great love of my life, and I would never have the capability or opportunity to love so deeply again. I had found peace in my new life and felt a profound curiosity, wondering what was next. I felt as though I was trust-falling, and my mind was open. Like a child on Christmas morning anticipating what's in the packages, I anticipated gleefully what was in store for me. I was delightfully surprised to find myself in a deep and meaningful relationship after letting go, listening to my emotional guidance system, and just enjoying the curiosity.

Each of us has a Higher Self, a calm, wise, loving inner voice that knows our path better than our logical mind ever could. I've come to understand that my Higher Self communicates not through loud warnings but through subtle nudges, deep knowings, and moments of inner peace. The more I slow down and get quiet, the more clearly I can hear her. Trusting my Higher Self has meant honoring my feelings, even when they didn't make sense to others. It's been one of the most liberating practices of my spiritual journey.

There's a difference between hoping something will work out and *knowing* it will. Knowing is a full-body sensation, a sense of alignment that needs no external validation. Over the years, I've learned to trust that feeling, even when it defies logic. When something feels expansive, light, or deeply exciting, it's usually a green light from my Higher Self. When it feels heavy, contracted, or draining, it's a loving redirection. This inner compass has never steered me wrong, and every time I listen, it gets stronger.

When we align and allow, manifestation comes easily. Manifestation isn't about wishing harder; it's about aligning our energy, beliefs, and actions with the life we want to live. It's a process of becoming. When we live from the energy of gratitude, worthiness, and trust, we naturally draw in experiences that reflect that state. Manifestation asks us to dream big, to hold beautiful visions for our lives, but also to let go of the "how" and "when." Our job is to plant the seeds, nourish them with belief, and trust that the harvest will come right on time.

One of the most humbling lessons has been learning to trust Divine Timing. Sometimes the waiting is not a punishment; it's a preparation. Sometimes the thing we want is still growing roots beneath the surface. Divine Timing teaches me that my timeline is not always the universe's timeline, and that's a good thing. The right things, aligned things, come when we are truly ready to receive them. Until then, I practice patience and gratitude for exactly where I am.

Recognizing the signs and synchronicities that show up along the journey is one of the most delightful parts of trusting the universe. A perfectly timed song lyric, a repeated number pattern, a stranger saying exactly what I needed to hear. These little "winks" remind me that I am seen, heard, and guided. When I'm open and paying attention, life feels like a conversation with the divine. It's comforting to know that even when I feel alone, I'm never truly navigating this path by myself.

Spirituality isn't about sitting back and waiting for life to happen *to* me; it's about actively co-creating my reality. I dream, I act, I surrender. It's a dance! Sometimes leading, sometimes following. Co-creation means taking inspired action when called, while still holding everything loosely enough to let miracles unfold. It's a partnership between me and the universe, one built on trust, alignment, and a deep respect for the mystery.

Finally, I've learned that protecting my energy is not selfish, it's essential. Who and what I allow into my space directly impacts my ability to stay connected to my Higher Self and to the flow of the universe. Energy hygiene means setting boundaries with love, clearing my space regularly (through nature, movement, or meditation), and being intentional about what I consume, whether it's conversations, media, or environments. By keeping my energetic field clear, I stay more aligned with the life I'm here to create.

Living with trust in the universe isn't about never having doubts or fears. It's about building a deep, unshakeable faith that even when I can't see the path ahead, I know I'm still being guided. It's a practice, one of remembering, over and over again, that I am supported, I am loved, and I am exactly where I need to be. The universe is always working behind the scenes, weaving a story more beautiful than you can imagine. Trust the unfolding.

Questions to ponder:

1. What would it feel like to truly trust that life is unfolding for your highest good?

2. If your thoughts shape your reality, what are you currently giving the most attention to?

3. When was the last time you noticed a sign or synchronicity that felt too perfect to be a coincidence, and what might it have been guiding you toward?

CHAPTER TWENTY-FOUR

Dating Frogs and Princes

Let's be honest, dating after loss, especially later in life, is a wild and vulnerable ride. It's strange terrain, especially when the last person I dated held such a permanent place in my heart. When Peter died, I didn't just lose my husband. I lost my best friend, my anchor, my daily rhythm. The house was silent, and the evenings stretched long and empty. I was lonely, yes—but more than that, I was aching for connection. For someone to witness me, to wrap their arms around me at the end of the day, and remind me that I was still lovable. Still wanted. Still here.

So, I jumped in. Fast. Too fast.

I downloaded the apps—those colorful icons full of possibility and awkward hope. And I did what so many of us do: I made profiles, swiped through faces, messaged strangers, tried to fill the cavern Peter left behind. Some of it was entertaining. Some of it was tragic. Most of it was a lesson.

Looking back, I can see that I was trying to outrun my grief with distraction, with chemistry, with anyone who would look at me like I was special again. But deep down, I wasn't ready. I was tender. I was untethered. And in that vulnerable space, I made choices I wouldn't make today.

I stayed too long in conversations that weren't kind. I excused red flags because I feared being alone more than I feared being misunderstood. I mistook attention for affection, and chemistry for compatibility. I dated men who weren't good for me because, at the time, I wasn't being very good to myself. I didn't yet know how to guard my peace or protect my energy. I didn't know how to tell the difference between butterflies and warning signs.

In truth, I had to step away. I had to sit myself down and say: *You're not broken, but you are bleeding. And dating while bleeding is only going to get messier.* I started learning about attachment patterns and recognized my own anxious tendencies—I was constantly looking for reassurance, for someone to make me feel secure, instead of finding that security within myself. It was a hard but necessary mirror to look into.

Dating as a widow is unlike anything else. You carry a love story in your heart even as you try to write a new one. There's guilt. There's comparison. There's fear of being hurt, of forgetting, of starting over. And yet, there's also this wild, beautiful hope that maybe, just maybe, you get another chance. I believe in that. I've lived that.

But the road to my prince had its share of frogs. And I say that without bitterness—every relationship, even the painful ones, taught me something about what I value, what I need, and most of all, how I want to feel in love: safe, seen, and deeply respected.

Perhaps I didn't fully realize how many elements of my relationship with Peter I had taken for granted. We shared an unspoken, fluid kind of love—steady, respectful, and safe— and I assumed that kind of connection was universal. I expected to be treated the way Peter had treated me.

What I hadn't yet learned was that expecting something isn't the same as **insisting** on it. It took me time—and a few hard lessons—to understand that I had to *require* the kind of love I deserved.

If you're stepping into dating after loss or later in life, here's what I want to say to you: take your time. Protect your heart without closing it off. Be curious, not desperate. Trust your gut—and if it feels off, it probably is. You are not too old, too damaged, or too late. You are worthy of great love, but the first love that matters is the one you offer yourself.

As I navigated the world of dating apps, I realized I needed to create some *rules of engagement*—not because I was trying to be rigid, but because I wanted to feel safe, physically and emotionally. And honestly, I didn't always follow my own rules (we'll get to that), but having them helped me feel like I had my own back.

Safety, for me, was non-negotiable. I wouldn't give out my phone number until I had a real sense of comfort chatting through the app. And even then, I learned the hard way that texting alone isn't enough. There's something powerful about hearing someone's voice. More than once, I thought I had a great connection through messages, only to finally talk on the phone and realize—yikes—we were on different planets. So I started suggesting a quick phone call, or, better yet, a video chat. It's a great way to confirm they're not using decade-old photos or borrowing someone else's dog for profile clout. A little FaceTime goes a long way!

And no matter how great the banter was, I *never* invited anyone to my home or told them where I lived. We always met in a public, neutral location. First dates were always short and sweet— "let's grab a coffee" or "a quick drink"—because, let's be honest, no one wants to be stuck at a two-hour dinner with someone who turns out to be...not your person. If the vibe was right, the date could naturally extend to dinner or a walk. But I kept the door open to exit gracefully.

I dated a handful of princes… and a *whole* lot of one-date frogs. I had no roadmap—just pure trial and error. Take one coffee date, for example. His profile photos showed a broad-shouldered, physically fit guy in his 50s. He looked sharp, confident, and active. We had a pleasant phone conversation, so I figured—okay, this could be promising. But when I walked into the coffee shop, I genuinely didn't recognize him. The man sitting at the table looked at least a decade older than the photos he'd posted. He appeared disheveled and tired, with five visible layers of shirts—yes, *five*—as if he were trying to create the illusion of bulk where there was none. Underneath all that fabric, he was painfully thin, and the vibrant energy he'd portrayed online was nowhere in sight.

It wasn't just the physical difference—it was the dissonance between who he *presented* himself to be and who he actually was. That's what stuck with me. Dating later in life means navigating a minefield of old profile pictures, exaggerated bios, and carefully curated personas. I don't fault people for wanting to present their best selves, but I do think we owe each other honesty. Because if we're looking for a real connection, it has to start with real representation.

Now, here's a pet peeve: ghosting. I know it's common, but I think it's lazy and unkind. If someone texted after a date and I wasn't feeling it, I'd reply with a simple, respectful message like, *"Thank you so much. It was nice to meet you, but I didn't feel the connection I was hoping for."* Period. It's not easy to be honest, but it's a reflection of your character. And truthfully, I wouldn't want to be left wondering—so I try not to leave someone else in that spot either. This was my response to Mr. Coffeehouse, to which he shared his disappointment. An hour later, he texted me again and said, "Friends with benefits?" I promptly blocked his number.

One trap I fell into more than once? Getting emotionally invested through long back-and-forth messaging before ever meeting. I'd be deep into conversations, swapping stories and building up an image of the person, only to meet in real life and feel absolutely nothing. When that happened, the disappointment hit harder. So eventually, I set a new rule: don't over-chat. A few exchanges are fine, but if someone's interested, they'll want to meet. If they keep messaging endlessly without making a plan, it's probably going nowhere.

This happened with a man I felt surprisingly comfortable with—at least at first. We chatted for weeks before finally making plans to meet. Because we'd built a friendly rhythm in our conversations, I felt safe enough to say yes to dinner instead of just a casual coffee. But the moment we met in person, I knew. There was zero connection. He lacked the confidence I'm naturally drawn to, and he was sweating so profusely I was genuinely concerned for his well-being.

It was uncomfortable, not because he was a bad person, but because the energy we had while chatting didn't translate at all in person. That's the risk of investing too much time before a face-to-face. Afterward, things got awkward. I knew it wasn't going anywhere and honestly, I think he did too—but he kept texting, kept engaging on my Facebook page, trying to keep the connection alive. Eventually, he crossed a line with some inappropriate comments, and I had to unfriend him. It wasn't mean—it was necessary. That experience reminded me how important it is to meet sooner rather than later, and to trust my instincts when something feels off.

In the early days of dating after Peter passed, I was so desperate to feel loved again that I sometimes tried to *make* something work, even when it was clear it wasn't meant to. I'd over-text, overthink, and over-give, trying to earn someone's interest. I thought if I just showed them how kind, funny, thoughtful, and "low-maintenance" I was, they'd see my worth. But let me tell you: when someone is meant for you, you won't need to convince them.

There's a big difference between showing up and chasing. When we chase, we often ignore our own needs just to keep someone else interested. We lean forward too much, hoping our effort will be mirrored back. But attraction doesn't work like that. The right person is drawn to your energy, your confidence, and your peace. They'll pursue *you* because you're showing up as your full, grounded, vibrant self, not because you're bending yourself into a pretzel to get their attention.

Eventually, I did meet someone and had a relationship that lasted far too long. A relationship with a man who had deep narcissistic tendencies. He chipped away at my confidence, constantly gaslighting me until I started to question my own instincts. I found myself chasing his approval, bending over backward for scraps of connection. I told myself that *some* attention and companionship was better than being alone and lonely. But I was wrong. So wrong. I deserved better.

One of the most painful red flags I ignored was how uncomfortable he was with my grief. He was even jealous of Peter. I couldn't talk about my late husband without feeling like I had to walk on eggshells. Instead of offering me a safe space to honor my past, he made me feel like I had to hide it. That left me feeling more alone than ever, even in a relationship.

My intuition was screaming at me the whole time, but I had gotten so used to tuning it out. Friends and family dropped subtle (and not-so-subtle) hints, but I couldn't hear them—not really. It wasn't until I caught him in an enormous, hurtful lie that I finally stopped explaining things away and cut ties. It hurt, but it was also a turning point. That relationship taught me a powerful lesson: being alone isn't the same as being lonely, and chasing someone who doesn't see your worth is the loneliest place of all.

So, here's the truth I had to sit with: if I felt like I was doing all the work to keep the conversation or relationship alive, it probably wasn't mutual. And if it's not mutual, it's not sustainable. I started asking myself, *"Do I feel chased or am I doing the chasing? Is there an equal and playful push and pull?"* And when I found myself chasing? I stepped back. Every time. That pause gave me space to remember what I truly want—a relationship where effort flows both ways.

I met a lovely man through Bumble. We chatted, exchanged numbers, and decided to meet for a hike. From the very beginning, he was a true gentleman: kind, respectful, and incredibly grounded. What struck me most was his peaceful energy—there was a quiet strength about him that made me feel safe and at ease. We quickly discovered a shared belief in something greater than ourselves, a spiritual connection that made our conversations feel almost sacred. We spoke about intention, purpose, healing, and the unseen ways life shapes us. Our values aligned in a way that felt rare and meaningful.

Over the course of five dates—hiking in nature, enjoying dinners, walking and talking for hours—I grew to deeply respect him. He listened with care. He showed up with integrity. And he honored my grief without trying to fix or avoid it. I truly cherished the space we created together. It was calm and kind and full of grace.

And yet, as much as I valued who he was and the comfort I felt in his presence, I didn't feel the kind of chemistry I knew I needed in a romantic partner. It was a hard truth to face. But I couldn't continue on, knowing I wasn't fully in it with my heart. I respected him—and our connection—too much to pretend. I had to walk away, for both of us.

It's hard to remain friends in situations like that. The loss of his companionship left a quiet ache. But choosing honesty was an act of care, not only for myself, but for him too. I hope he knows how much I admired him—and how grateful I am for the time we shared.

Even in the midst of dating, you can think that you have found "Mr Right." Or in the case of one hottie I met on Bumble, "Dr. Right."But what I didn't see coming was the heartbreak. Dr. So-and-So seemed to follow all the rules I had set for myself. We chatted on the app, and he felt too good to be true, even after we exchanged numbers. I insisted on a Zoom call before meeting in person, and the moment our faces appeared on screen, I felt a connection I hadn't experienced before. He was healthy and fit, wildly successful, articulate, spiritually aware—and he poured on the compliments, spoonfeeding my love language like he had read the manual.

We made plans to meet for dinner that weekend. When I arrived at the restaurant, he ran toward me like we were long-lost lovers in a movie scene. He wrapped himself around me, kissed me as though we'd been in love for years. I literally dropped my purse in the parking lot. We went inside but barely touched our food—the chemistry was electric. Afterward, we continued the date privately... and it lasted until lunchtime the next day.

It all felt so easy, so natural—like we'd known each other for lifetimes. There was a magnetic pull that neither of us could explain. I now understand that what I was experiencing was love bombing, but at the time, it felt like fate.

In the two weeks that followed, we saw each other 11 more times. We cooked for one another, went on hikes, lingered over breakfasts and dinners, and spent nights tangled in sheets. He even walked my dog and shoveled my driveway. There were "I love you's" exchanged within days, and while it felt fast, it also felt undeniable. Maybe we both had attachment wounds we hadn't healed. Maybe we were two lonely people clinging to the idea of a soulmate.

But just as quickly as it began, the temperature shifted. After a couple of months, I could feel him pulling away. When I gently confronted him, he told me his life was chaotic, that he needed to focus on work. And then I learned the truth—he had found another heart to break.

My heart ached in a way I hadn't expected. It wasn't just about him—it was the sting of hope being snatched away just when I thought I had found something real. That experience jolted me awake. I knew I needed to stop dating and turn inward. I had to heal, to restore trust in myself, and reconnect with the parts of me that didn't need someone else to feel whole.

Dating after loss, especially later in life, is not for the faint of heart. It's filled with highs and heartbreaks, self-discovery and soul-searching. I met kind men, confusing men, emotionally unavailable men, and a few who truly touched my heart, even if just for a season. Each encounter taught me something: about boundaries, about trust, about the kind of love I was no longer willing to settle for. But most importantly, it revealed how desperately I needed to come home to myself. Before I could build something healthy and lasting with someone else, I had to learn how to offer that love, comfort, and companionship to the one person I would be with forever—me.

Questions to ponder:

1. Have you ever ignored your own intuition in a relationship? What did it feel like in your body or spirit when something was "off?"

2. Have you ever stayed in a relationship simply because being alone felt too scary or painful? How did that serve—or hurt—you in the long run?

3. Have you experienced heartbreak? What lessons did that heartbreak teach you about love, attachment, and healing?

CHAPTER TWENTY-FIVE

Dating Myself

After all the swipes, first dates, flings, heartbreaks, and hopeful beginnings, I realized something essential: I had been so focused on finding the right partner that I hadn't stopped to be the right partner to myself.

The space between heartbreak and healing can be fertile ground if you let it, and I knew I needed to tend to myself before inviting anyone else to plant roots with me. So, I took a breather, deleted the dating apps, and took a conscious break from dating, not out of bitterness, but out of love. I made a quiet but powerful decision: I was going to commit to myself for a while.

This chapter is about that choice, to date myself first, and the peace, clarity, and self-respect that came with it.

After Dr. Love Bomb disappeared, I knew I needed to hit pause. Not just a casual break, but a full stop. For more than four months, I didn't go on a single date. No flirty banter, no awkward small talk over coffee, no endless waiting for a text that might never come.

It wasn't always easy. There were lonely moments, vulnerable realizations, and quiet evenings that stretched longer than I liked. But slowly, I found something beautiful and new: comfort in my own company. I treated myself with care and compassion, like I wanted to be cared for by a partner. I honored what I'd been through, and I gave myself space to heal fully, not just from the last heartbreak, but from years of putting someone else's needs before my own.

I wanted to rediscover who I was when no one else was watching, to nurture the parts of me that had been overshadowed by the need for connection. To remember what made me feel grounded, joyful, and complete. I was still carrying pieces of unhealed hurt, unclear boundaries, and a longing for companionship that sometimes clouded my judgment. I needed space, not just from dating, but from the noise of it all.

I had been so focused on finding love that I hadn't truly paused to love myself in the ways I needed. Love myself? I'm not sure I even liked myself. I gave myself the gift of stillness. I turned inward, asking deeper questions: What do I truly want? What do I deserve? Who am I authentically?

I found ways to spend time discovering and remembering what it felt like to be whole. I decided to date myself, invest in myself, and fall in love with the life I was building—whether or not someone else showed up to share it.

Every day, I gifted myself the luxury of spending hours on my backyard swing listening to inspirational podcasts, devouring chapters of three or four books at a time. I napped on that swing, cried on it, laughed with friends on the phone, and let myself heal. It became my sanctuary, the place where I gave myself full permission to rediscover what I liked about me.

I found that my relationships with friends and family grew deeper as I relaxed into the comfort of being with myself—no longer desperately searching for love elsewhere, but instead turning toward the love that had always been there. First in my family, then in my friendships, and finally, within myself.

I leaned into being alone, not in a lonely or self-pitying way, but in an intentional, healing way. I wanted to understand why I'd been chasing connection so urgently, and what it was I thought I was missing. Four months may not sound like much, but when you've been dating regularly—swiping, chatting, prepping for dates, picking out the right outfit, rehearsing conversation starters, and hoping for a spark—it feels like a deep exhale.

That quiet, that stillness, gave me space to really look inward. I started showing up for myself in ways I'd reserved for others. I began asking myself the hard questions and offering the kind of compassion I'd been so quick to extend to everyone but me. I wasn't just single, I was healthy, healing, and beginning to rewrite the story I'd been telling myself about love, worth, and what it means to truly be ready to share myself with someone else.

I lit candles just for me. I cooked beautiful meals and set the table even if I was the only one sitting at it. I took long walks and played my favorite music without compromise. I gave myself permission to rest, to cry, to laugh at silly things, and to mend. I paid attention to what made me feel good— what sparked joy, and what drained me. I practiced self-care like it was my job and, slowly, I began to feel more restored. Not because someone else was filling my needs and desires, but because I was finally tending to my own.

There's something powerful about not needing to be chosen. I had spent so much energy trying to be "good

173

enough" for someone else, contorting myself to be wanted, lovable, less complicated. But now, I was learning to love all of me, not just the shiny parts, but the messy, unsure, still-healing parts too. I wasn't editing my personality or opinions to be more palatable.

I began to ask myself deeper questions: What do I really want in a partner? What do I truly value in a relationship? Who would I attract if I loved myself with full conviction? Who would be drawn to me if I stood firmly in my truth and didn't dim my light?

During that sacred spring, I grounded myself in my faith and spirituality. I revisited my core values. I made peace with my past and forgave myself for the choices I had made while grieving and seeking companionship. I realized that clarity often comes in the quiet, and I had finally given myself enough stillness to listen. My confidence grew. My sense of self deepened. And I stopped asking, "Will someone love me?" and started affirming, "I already do."

By the time I decided to download the apps again, I felt different. Stronger. Clearer. Not in a "I've got it all figured out" way, but in a "I know who I am now" kind of way. I wasn't searching for someone to complete me; I was inviting someone to join me in a life I already loved.

I had stronger boundaries, not as a wall to keep people out, but as a way to honor myself and protect the peace I had worked so hard to create. I became rooted in my own worth, and I was no longer afraid to walk away from something that didn't feel right. I knew what I deserved, and I wouldn't settle for less.

My self-respect grew in ways I hadn't anticipated. It was no longer just a concept—it was a feeling in my body, a posture I carried, a boundary I held without apology. I stopped saying yes when I meant maybe. I stopped chasing closure or approval. I stopped shrinking.

For the first time in a long time, I felt truly at home with myself in a way that brought me extreme peace. And when I did eventually open the door to dating again, I knew I would walk in with my head high, my voice steady, and my heart aligned with the love I knew I deserved. I was no longer willing to chase chemistry if it came at the expense of peace. I wanted connection, but only if it allowed me to remain fully, unapologetically me.

I had become more grounded, more honest, and more aware of what I truly needed in a partner. I wasn't looking to be saved, entertained, or validated. I was open—but from a place of clarity, not craving. And when I decided I was ready to explore dating again, as the best version of myself, the most unexpected and wonderful thing happened.

Questions to ponder:

1. If you planned a date just for you, no one to impress, no one to accommodate, what would it include?

2. What's one thing you can do this week to "date yourself," to offer yourself attention, delight, or tenderness without needing a reason?

3. Have you ever confused wanting to be chosen with wanting to be loved?

CHAPTER TWENTY-SIX

Choosing to Bloom

There comes a point when hiding who we are just feels too heavy. When we realize we've been shrinking—biting our tongue, second-guessing our instincts, dimming our light—to stay comfortable or keep the peace. But comfort isn't the same as peace. And blooming? Blooming is what happens when we choose to show up as ourselves, without apology. This chapter is about that choice. About stepping out from behind the smaller version of ourselves we've learned to live in, and into something fuller, freer, and more true. Not louder. Not flashier. Just honest. Just real. Just *you*.

When I talk about *shrinking*, I'm not referring to physical size—I'm talking about the subtle (and sometimes not-so-subtle) ways we make ourselves smaller to feel safer or more accepted. It can look like biting your tongue when you have something important to say. Downplaying your accomplishments so others won't feel uncomfortable. Hiding your grief, your joy, your truth—because you're afraid of being "too much" or not enough. Shrinking is what we do when we silence parts of ourselves to fit into spaces that were never meant to hold our whole, vibrant being. It's a survival mechanism, often rooted in past experiences or societal expectations, but it's not where we're meant to live.

In the early days of my caregiving journey, I often found myself shrinking, not out of weakness, but out of habit. I would swallow my exhaustion, soften the edges of my truth, and package my pain into digestible bits for the comfort of others. I worried that being too honest about the rage, the grief, the sacred tenderness of watching my husband fade would make people uncomfortable. So, I edited myself. I smiled when I wanted to scream. I nodded through well-meaning clichés like "You're so strong," or "At least you still have him," even though I sometimes felt like I was slowly drowning. I believed that if I kept the messiness hidden, I could still belong. That I could make everyone else more at ease, even if it meant contorting myself into a smaller, more agreeable version.

But somewhere along the way, I realized that shrinking didn't serve anyone—not me, and certainly not the people who needed to hear the truth. When I began to share openly, first in conversations, then on paper, and finally with the world, I felt myself bloom. Not in one sudden burst, but like a slow unfolding. Each time I spoke a raw truth aloud—about love, loss, resentment, tears in the dark—I reclaimed a piece of myself. I stopped apologizing for the depth of my story and started honoring it. What had once felt like a burden became a bridge to others who were silently carrying the same weight. By choosing to bloom, I stepped into a space where my vulnerability became my superpower. I wasn't just surviving anymore; I was giving others permission to speak, to feel, to grieve, and to find hope. And in doing so, I found the fullest, most radiant version of myself.

That experience taught me something far bigger than how to navigate caregiving; it taught me how to live. I realized that shrinking to fit is a habit rooted in fear: fear of rejection, discomfort, and being misunderstood. But blooming? Blooming is a choice rooted in self-trust. Now, I carry that lesson with me everywhere I go. Whether I'm in a boardroom, on a hiking trail, meeting someone new, or simply showing up publicly, I practice being unapologetically me. I speak up, even when it takes bravery. I share my beliefs, even if they're not popular. I trust that being authentic, even when it's vulnerable or uncomfortable, is not only a gift to myself but an invitation to others to do the same. It's no longer about being palatable or pleasing. It's about being real. And that, I've learned, is where true connection and joy begin. It's a place where pride in myself and peace meet.

To bloom is to choose authenticity; not the curated, performative kind, but the messy, radiant truth of who you really are. It's brave. It's vulnerable. And it's deeply freeing. Authenticity doesn't always mean revealing everything; sometimes it means choosing what not to hide anymore. Sometimes it's knowing what to share and with whom.

In this season of my life, I feel it: I am blooming. Not into someone new, but into who I've always been underneath the weight of expectations, roles, and grief. There is peace in allowing myself to take up space. To love out loud. To be both softer and stronger.

American poet, painter, essayist, and playwright E.E. Cummings said, *"It takes courage to grow up and become who you really are."*

This kind of blooming doesn't ask for permission. It's the reward of doing the inner work. Of listening inward and choosing to show up real instead of perfect. And when we bloom, really bloom, we give silent permission to others to do the same.

Shrinking may feel safe but, over time, it costs us far more than we realize. When we shrink, we silence parts of ourselves to avoid discomfort, ours or someone else's. We hold back joy to seem modest. We bite our tongues to keep the peace. We hide our grief to avoid being "too much." We tuck away our dreams because they might seem unrealistic or inconvenient. But each time we do, we chip away at the full expression of who we are. Shrinking, over time, becomes a habit, one that feels like self-protection, but often ends up as self-abandonment.

The price? We become strangers to ourselves. We attract relationships built on performance and fraud, not presence or authenticity. We lose creative spark, clarity, and confidence. And, perhaps most painfully, we begin to believe we are only lovable in smaller doses.

There is also a grief in shrinking: a subtle, aching kind, because deep down, we know we were made for more. We can feel it in the quiet moments: the unspoken words, the hidden laughter, the instinct we ignored, the path we didn't follow. Shrinking isn't just about what we avoid; it's about what we miss. The connection, the growth, the chance to be fully alive.

To bloom, we must first recognize how we've been folding ourselves up to fit into spaces that were never meant to contain us. When something feels heavy, constricting, or off, that's our emotional guidance system speaking up. And if we listen, it can lead us toward choices that feel more honest, freeing, and true to who we are. It requires unlearning and releasing the roles and expectations that told us our fullness was too loud, too messy, too sensitive, too much. Blooming asks us to stop apologizing for our existence and start honoring it.

There is no peace in pretending. The peace comes from being fully, wholly, and blatantly you. Living authentically doesn't mean rejecting the world; it means refusing to reject yourself in order to be accepted by the world.

I've learned through experience that authenticity begins with a pause to honor myself, a moment of inward listening. It's asking, *What feels true for me?* before responding, committing, or compromising. It's recognizing when we're slipping into autopilot or old roles just to make others comfortable. Authentic living invites us to notice the subtle ways we perform, please, or protect, and to replace those habits with presence, honesty, and intention.

It's not easy. We're conditioned from an early age to conform and to blend in, to be agreeable, to follow the script. We learn which parts of ourselves are celebrated and which ones are met with silence, criticism, or distance. So, we shape-shift. We hustle for belonging. But that kind of acceptance always comes at a cost, because it's based on who we pretend to be, not who we really are.

To live authentically is to rewrite that script. It's choosing your voice over approval. Your values over validation. Your path over perfection. This isn't about being defiant, it's about being aligned. Living this way might mean saying "no" more often. It might mean showing up without a mask. It might mean loving differently, dressing differently, speaking differently than what others expect. It might mean disappointing people who liked the edited version of you. But the reward is immeasurable: peace, freedom, and the deep, grounding joy of coming home to yourself.

Questions to ponder:

1. Where in your life have you been shrinking to feel safe, accepted, or agreeable?

2. What do you need to give yourself permission to do, feel, or become?

3. Who in your life supports your blooming — and who still prefers the smaller version of you?

CHAPTER TWENTY-SEVEN

Unexpected Love

In the world of dating, people often suggest, "Make a list of what you want in a partner." And, I did. Clarity matters. But what I learned, through experience, not just advice, is that before you go searching for someone who checks all your boxes, you've got to become the kind of person who *matches* that list. Not perfectly. Not by pretending. But by genuinely growing into the energy you want to attract. It's not about chasing or performing, it's about aligning with who you really are, and letting that truth do the attracting.

When I considered each of the important traits I was searching for in someone else—honest communication—integrity—kindness—curiosity—emotional availability—I had to ask myself, "Am I living these qualities?" Because without that alignment, there's no real energetic connection. It's like tuning your radio to the wrong frequency; you just can't find each other.

I didn't want someone to complete me. That kind of thinking belongs to old fairy tales and co-dependent patterns.

I wanted someone to *complement* me. Someone with their own fullness, who could meet me in mine. Someone to share life with, not fill a gap. And that shifted things in an eye-opening way. The desperation that had once quietly hummed underneath previous dating attempts, the part of me that hoped someone might rescue me from loneliness, was gone.

Instead, I found myself *curious*. Not needy. Curious about who I might meet. Curious about what would unfold. I began to approach dating with lightness, not with dread. I wasn't anxiously checking my phone or over-analyzing messages. I didn't feel like I was auditioning anymore. I was showing up as myself, and that was enough.

You should be excited to go on the date, not filled with anxiety. I used to think anxiety before a date was normal, just part of the process. But anxiety is often a signal. It shows up when something in us is still unhealed, when we're afraid we're not enough, when we're trying to be chosen rather than choosing. It's the vibration of fear, and guess what? You'll likely end up sitting across the table from someone holding the same vibration. Like attracts like, not just in lifestyle or interests, but energetically.

If you're holding fear, you'll draw in fear. If you're anchored in self-worth, you'll draw in someone who respects that. And that energetic resonance is everything. When you do the work to heal, to soften, to come home to yourself, the people you draw in shift. That's what happened with Jonathan.

One of the first things I admired about Jonathan was his communication. Not just the frequency of it, though, yes, he texted back like a grown man with manners, but the quality of it. He was clear, open, and honest from the beginning. He didn't try to impress me or play it cool. He said what he meant, and he meant what he said. It's what allowed our connection to take root. It's what kept me curious to learn more about him.

Early on, he told me what he was looking for, and just as importantly, what he *wasn't* sure about yet. And when unexpected feelings started to show up, feelings he hadn't planned on having, he didn't run or shut down. He shared them. Honestly. Tenderly. Even when it felt vulnerable. Even when he wasn't sure what they meant yet. He didn't promise things he couldn't give, and he didn't fake confidence he didn't feel. Instead, he let me into his thought process, his hopes, his fears, and all the questions in between.

Eventually, when it turned into love and he knew it, he told me that, too. Not with grand gestures or sweeping statements, but with the kind of honesty that carries real weight: *I love you. I didn't expect to. I wasn't sure I was ready. But I am.*

That kind of truth-telling, that kind of self-awareness and vulnerability, isn't always common, especially early in dating. But it was everything. It matched what I had been practicing in myself. I wasn't interested in surface connection anymore. I wanted emotional safety. Clarity. A partner who could meet me in the deeper places. And because Jonathan showed up that way, our connection had space to take root and grow. Gently, honestly, and with trust at the center.

All the work I did on myself during my sabbatical from dating created the space for us to find each other, not just logistically, but energetically. It wasn't about chasing, convincing, or proving. It was about *recognizing*. Two people meeting in their fullness. That's what happens when you stop searching for someone to save you and instead stand steady in the love you've already cultivated within yourself.

The funny thing is, when you're finally steady in yourself, the person who shows up might totally surprise you. I was *highly* attracted to Jonathan, but I figured he was a player, and definitely not relationship material. I never imagined we'd end up building something real.

In fact, when Jonathan and I met, I told myself, told everyone, actually, *this isn't sustainable*. We had almost nothing in common. He blasted hard rock; I played feel-good pop. He spent hours immersed in video games; I barely knew how to hold a controller. I'm neat, organized, and borderline obsessive. He is… not. Picture this: me, channeling my inner Martha Stewart with everything in its place, and Jonathan, a full-on Dennis the Menace, happily leaving a trail of playful mess behind him. I love morning workouts and long walks in nature. Jonathan prefers city energy and has never once considered a plank or push-up part of his ideal day. So naturally, we both assumed this connection, however fun or interesting, wasn't going anywhere. But the universe seemed to have other plans.

What I thought was incompatibility turned out to be irrelevance. Because beneath all those differences, beneath the playlists and habits and environments, we shared something deeper: *respect. Curiosity. A desire to grow.* A willingness to talk through anything, even the uncomfortable stuff. We had the same communication style: open, direct, and emotionally honest. And perhaps even more importantly, we both *wanted* to keep learning each other, instead of changing each other.

Jonathan says it all the time: *"We're easy."* And he's right. We didn't come into each other's lives to tick boxes. We came in to soften each other, to balance each other, to build something rooted in our own unexpected harmony.

Sure, at first, the glue was the electricity, that undeniable chemistry that neither of us saw coming. It was strong. Magnetic. And it would've been easy to stop there. But we didn't. We kept exploring. Planning things together. Finding common ground in our future, even if our pasts looked nothing alike. We merged friend groups. Took trips to places we love. Introduced each other to things we never thought we'd enjoy, and ended up enjoying them just because we were doing them *together*.

The more I looked, the more I realized we *did* have things in common. Maybe not hobbies, but deeper threads—a desire to be seen, a love of laughter, loyalty, passion, and presence. Those are the things that make relationships sustainable.

The truth is, having everything in common doesn't mean a relationship will work. And having nothing in common doesn't mean it won't. What matters is *how* you show up. What you're willing to offer. How open you are to being surprised. Jonathan and I are very different. And yet… we are absolutely right for each other.

The second connector for us, right behind communication, was our immature, completely ridiculous sense of humor. We both have this silly, juvenile streak that is often met with eye rolls by past partners, friends and family. But with each other? It's celebrated. We're talking full-on dad jokes, bad puns, goofy voices, and practical jokes. We sneak around corners trying to scare each other, poke fun at one another, send absurd texts just to get a laugh, and somehow find humor in the weirdest moments. Our shared silliness is like our own secret language—pure, unfiltered joy.

I think we both felt relieved to be with someone who didn't just *tolerate* that part of us, but actually *matched* it. It's not polished or impressive, it's real. And it keeps things light, especially when life gets heavy. We're a perfect fit in this way: two grown-ups with the playful spirits of 12-year-olds, and we wouldn't have it any other way. We're undeniable flirts, and that playful spark between us keeps a constant smile painted on our faces, like we're in on the best secret the world doesn't know yet.

There's something especially healing about finding someone you can laugh with *after* loss. After grief strips life down to its bare bones, joy becomes sacred. I know what it's like to take life seriously, because I had to. But now? We don't want to live in constant heaviness. We say "so what" more often, let the little stuff go, and choose to laugh instead of spiral. Our humor isn't just entertainment; it's a way of reclaiming joy. Of reminding each other that we're still here, still capable of lightness, still able to be silly and free. And that's its own kind of miracle.

But what makes that joy feel even safer, more rooted, is knowing I can also bring my sorrow. One of the qualities I most admire in Jonathan is his complete and compassionate understanding of my grief. Before him, I dated men who were, quite honestly, jealous of Peter. Even though he had passed, they treated my memories as competition. They didn't know how to hold space for the love I still carried, or the moments when that love would suddenly resurface in the form of tears, silence, or stories that needed to be told again. Jonathan is different.

From the very beginning, he embraced my grief, not just intellectually, but emotionally and physically. He never tried to fix it. He never made it about himself. He simply showed up. There are still times, out of nowhere, when a song plays, or I see a photo, or a memory sweeps in like a wave, and I cry. And in those moments, Jonathan doesn't flinch. He offers his hand. His chest. His presence. He becomes the place I can safely land.

He once said to me, "You didn't have a fight and break up. Peter died. And you loved him." That sentence still lives in my heart. Because he *gets it*. He understands that love doesn't end just because life does. And he's never asked me to let go of Peter to make room for him. He knows the room was always there.

I will always love Peter. And Jonathan not only accepts that, he honors it. That kind of emotional maturity, that kind of steady love, is rare. It takes strength to stand beside someone who is still holding space for another, and never feel threatened. But Jonathan's heart is big enough to hold it all—my past, my memories, my pain, my dreams, and my joy.

I admire him so deeply for that. And I'm endlessly grateful for the safe space he's created, where I can cry if I need to, laugh through the memories, speak Peter's name freely, and continue to celebrate the man who shaped so much of who I am. That kind of safety? It's a gift. One I'll never stop cherishing.

Love didn't show up the way I imagined, but it showed up exactly how I needed. Not to fix me, not to replace what I lost, but to meet me in my fullness. To laugh with me, cry with me, surprise me, and build something new beside the old. With Jonathan, I didn't fall into love, I *chose* it. Over time, with open eyes and a steady heart. Our connection may have started with chemistry and curiosity, but what holds us together is so much more: honesty, humor, deep respect, and a sacred kind of spaciousness that allows both Peter's memory and our future to coexist.

Love, when it's right, doesn't ask you to shrink. It invites you to expand. And in Jonathan, I found a partner who lets me do just that: grow, grieve, laugh, and live fully. Unexpected love, yes. But meant to be, and deeply, truly cherished.

Questions to ponder:

1. In what ways has grief shaped your understanding of love and connection?

2. What qualities do you want in a partner, and are you actively nurturing those same qualities in yourself?

3. Are you allowing yourself to feel joy again, even after deep loss? What does joy look like for you now?

CHAPTER TWENTY-EIGHT

Blending Hearts and Homes

If you read the introduction, you already know the story of how Jonathan proposed—on a beach at sunset, with sand between our toes, my daughter recording and my son-in-law behind the camera, snapping away. It was dreamy and awkward and perfect, just like us. It felt easy to say yes, not only to Jonathan, but to a future I never expected to have. But what you don't know yet is what led to that moment and the surprising moments that kept unfolding in the most serendipitous ways.

When I think about how Jonathan and I met, it's hard not to see the hand of something greater at play—universal timing, divine humor, or maybe just a really smart Bumble algorithm. We had both expanded our search areas, quite literally widening the map. Jonathan even expanded his age range, something he admits he didn't usually do. I'm six years older than he is, and normally, he dated younger women.

On my end, I had a hard-and-fast rule: swipe left on anyone with kids still living at home. I had raised my three children, helped raise two stepchildren, and was deep in the beautiful chaos of grandmotherhood. I wasn't looking to revisit high school years. And yet... Jonathan slipped through. His son was fourteen. Somehow, we found each other anyway.

There were plenty of reasons we *shouldn't* have matched—timing, life stages, preferences, all the little filters we set when we think we know what we need. But connection doesn't always follow logic. It follows resonance. And there was something about him that drew me in, something steady, curious, and kind. We made each other laugh right away.

And when he mentioned his father was living with Alzheimer's in a memory care facility, I had a moment where my heart paused. That alone could've sent me running. I had *lived* that life. I had written about it, spoken about it, *survived* it. It wasn't something I wanted to re-enter. But instead of turning away, I leaned in. Not because I wanted to take it on again, but because his presence felt like something I could trust. He wasn't asking for help. He was sharing his life.

Looking back, I see how many little "no's" we would've said if we had been swiping on autopilot. If either of us had stuck to our usual filters, we never would have met. And yet, when I think of how easily life flows with him now, how we move through each day with love and laughter and just enough chaos, it all feels so wildly meant to be. Not perfect. Not expected. But *right*. Life has a way of delivering the exact person you need when you've finally done the work to be ready.

Just like our relationship, the next chapter of our life together began serendipitously, but with open hearts. We had casually started dreaming about a house we might share someday. The plan was loose and far off. We figured we'd move in together after Jonathan's son graduated from high school in a few years. There was no pressure, no timeline. Just a kind of playful visioning. A dreaming expedition.

He expanded his home search on Zillow slightly outside our intended area—just a small adjustment, one click, like he had done when he expanded his age range and location that day we found each other. And, once again, that tiny expansion led to something we never saw coming: our perfect house. It wasn't in the neighborhood we thought we wanted, but it was *exactly* what we needed. As soon as we walked in, we knew. It felt like ours. Not mine. Not his. *Ours.* We bought that home in December, and two months later, Jonathan proposed.

It all sounds fast on paper. But in my heart, it felt like the most natural unfolding. There was no pressure, no overthinking, no fear. Just that quiet emotional knowing I had come to trust—*this feels right.* It always has. We didn't go searching hard. We just stayed open. And life kept meeting us with more than we thought to ask for.

As our relationship blossomed, there was no trepidation. No uneasiness. Just… peace. I kept checking in with myself, listening closely to what I call my emotional guidance system—the quiet wisdom inside that lets me know when something feels aligned. And every time I tuned in, the answer was the same: *this feels good.* Not the butterflies kind of good, not the swept-away high that fizzles out. This was the kind of good that feels like exhaling. Like coming home. Like not having to perform or protect or prove.

There was a steadiness to our connection, a simplicity in the way we moved through each new phase—dating, deepening, sharing more of our lives. We didn't have to push or force or convince. There was no script to follow, no fear to soothe. Just a soft unfolding. And with every step forward, my heart said yes. Not out of hope or longing, but because it felt undeniably right. That kind of ease doesn't come from magic. It comes from trust—trust in myself, trust in what I've learned, and trust in the love that showed up when I stopped chasing and started simply *being, authentically.*

While our love was easy, packing up the house where I had lived for over twenty years felt like sorting through layers of a lifetime. Every drawer I opened, every closet shelf, held not just things, but memories. Peter's laugh in the kitchen. Family dinners with our blended family. The quiet nights when caregiving consumed everything and I would collapse into bed, exhausted but holding on. That house had seen it all—joy, heartbreak, love, loss, and everything in between. It held echoes of children's footsteps, milestones, grief, and the woman I used to be.

Some boxes were easy—old linens, unused gadgets, the clutter we all collect. But others? Others stopped me in my tracks. A photo tucked into a book. A note in Peter's handwriting. I let myself feel it all. I didn't rush. I cried when I needed to, smiled when something warm surfaced, and whispered thanks more than once to the walls around me.

When everything was finally packed, the rooms stood empty, but not hollow. There was a stillness, sacred, somehow. I walked through one last time, running my hand along the banister, pausing in the doorway of our old bedroom, standing in the kitchen where so much life had happened. And then I stood at the front door with the key in my hand, heart full and aching all at once. Closing that door for the last time wasn't just an ending. It was quiet, wholehearted permission to begin again.

Walking into our new home with Jonathan felt like walking into a fresh chapter we were writing together in real time. There was no lingering hesitation, no feeling of trying to fit into someone else's space. It was ours from the start. We had so many conversations before we moved in about what we both needed, what we both loved, how we wanted to live together, not just *coexist*. Our styles, both lifestyle and design-wise, couldn't be more different. I'm clean, orderly. Jonathan…isn't. He's creative chaos and has been a bachelor Dad for a decade. But somehow, it worked.

We laughed a lot through the process, negotiating over throw pillows, furniture, and paint colors, deciding where plates and glasses should live, and whether or not his movie posters could stay in the living room. (They could not.) There was such joy in it, even in the compromises. Because it was never really about the stuff. It was about building a life where both of us belonged.

What surprised me most wasn't just how much fun it was, but how *easy* it felt. We weren't blending two lives by force. We were creating something new. Something that reflected both of us, with space for growth, for love, and for all the little things that make a home feel alive. There was a quiet thrill in the everyday dreaming of where to put the garden, what kind of dinners we'd cook, and who we'd invite over. The house itself is beautiful, yes, but the most beautiful part was what it represented: a future we never saw coming, unfolding one ordinary, extraordinary day at a time.

Even as we built something new, there was never a question about bringing Peter along with us. His presence is part of who I am, part of what shaped the love I'm capable of giving now. In our new home, there's a framed photo of him in the dining room and an urn on the mantle that holds his ashes. We didn't tuck him away in a box or a closet. Peter is with us, in memory, in spirit, and in story. It's a symbol of how love continues, even as life moves forward.

Jonathan never made me choose. He never asked me to silence the past to make him more comfortable in the present. Instead, he made room for it. He understood that honoring Peter wasn't about clinging, it was about respect, about integration, about the beauty of a life fully lived. There's such peace in that, such wholeness. I didn't have to shut a door on my history to open one to my future.

And maybe that's what made everything feel so easy. We weren't pretending the past didn't exist. We were acknowledging it, blessing it, and letting it walk beside us as we built something new. This home, this love, this chapter, it's not a replacement. It's a continuation. One filled with laughter, intention, healing, and the sweet, quiet truth that nothing real is ever lost. It just changes form.

That same respect and acceptance we have for our shared past extends to honoring who we are as individuals, recognizing that our independence is a vital part of the life we're creating together. We're two distinct individuals, each with our own passions, hobbies, and rhythms. While we share a life and build a future together, we also honor the importance of having separate interests that keep us grounded and fulfilled on our own. He dives into his gaming worlds, and I cherish my quiet mornings enjoying meditation, a book, or gardening. We celebrate those differences, knowing they enrich our relationship rather than diminish it.

Respecting each other's outside activities isn't just about space, it's about trust and support. It means encouraging Jonathan to spend time with his friends or family without feeling tethered, and him understanding when I need my own time to recharge. This balance keeps our connection vibrant and healthy, reminding us that love doesn't mean losing ourselves. Instead, it's about coming together as whole people, each bringing our full selves to the partnership.

This balance of honoring our individual needs set the foundation for the deeper blending of our lives—where friends, family, and shared moments naturally came together with grace and ease. Meeting Jonathan's friends, being welcomed with open arms, and sharing laughter over meals felt easy and genuine.

Likewise, seeing him connect effortlessly with my friends, children, stepchildren, and grandbabies brought a new kind of fullness to our lives. It wasn't just about merging social calendars; it was about weaving together the people who mattered most, creating a larger, richer community where we both belonged. That ease, that flow of connection, was yet another reminder that this life wasn't something I had to build alone, it was something we were creating together, piece by joyful piece.

Building a life with Jonathan has been a journey of gentle unfolding where ease, acceptance, and love create the foundation. From expanding our horizons in unexpected ways to blending homes, honoring the past while embracing the future, and weaving our families and friends into one vibrant community, everything has felt natural and whole.

Now, as we plan not only a wedding but also the life we want to build together, there's a thrilling sense of possibility in the air, a readiness to step fully into this new chapter of life. And quietly, through our actions and the way we show up, we offer a gentle reminder to others that hope and healing are possible, even after profound loss. True connection isn't about perfection or rushing, it's about showing up fully, with openness and trust, ready to bloom in the space we create together.

ONE LAST THOUGHT

From My Heart to Yours

Dear Beloved Reader,

If you've made it to these final pages, please know this: I am so deeply honored you walked this journey with me. Thank you for showing up—for yourself, for your healing, and for the quiet unfolding of your own story.

Perhaps the most unexpected gift of finding joy is how it becomes light for others. We don't inspire people by pretending to have it all together; we inspire them by showing what it looks like to fall apart, rise slowly, and choose to bloom anyway. When we live openly, when we share our stories—the hard—the vulnerable—the healing, we invite others into their own courage.

I think often of Peter and our journey. I've told our story with raw honesty and transparency: the love, the laughter, the loss, and everything in between. Not because it was easy to share, but because it was *real*. And in that realness, I've seen people soften. I've watched others feel less alone. I've witnessed how one honest voice can echo into someone else's quiet ache and remind them: *you're not the only one.*

That's what it means to be a beacon of hope, not to have escaped the darkness, but to have walked through it, carrying a light that others can follow.

In this chapter of my life, I feel that light inside me. Not because everything is perfect, but because I am at peace. I am at home in myself, with no regrets. I am no longer trying to prove, fix, or strive. I am simply being. And that is more than enough.

There is much more life for me to live. These lessons I have experienced so far in my life are mere chapters of my entire story. I'm eagerly anticipating the coming pages and lessons. This is what joy looks like for me now:

Laughing louder and loving freely.

Saying yes to what feels true.

Saying no without guilt.

Practicing self-care deliberately.

Choosing joy without explanation.

Listening to and trusting my emotional guidance system.

Showing up with a heart that's soft from healing, not hardened by pain.

And leaving a legacy I approve of.

If this book has offered anything, I hope it's permission.

Permission to feel deeply.

To find joy every single day.

To live with no regrets.

To trust your becoming.

And to know that wherever you are on your journey, even if it doesn't feel like blooming yet, you are growing something beautiful.

You are not too sensitive.
You are not too much.
You are not too late.
You are not alone.

Keep blooming.
Much Love,
Lisa

ABOUT THE AUTHOR

Lisa Marshall is a speaker, writer, and advocate who lives by her mantra "Find joy, no regrets." Known for her motivating optimism, warmth, and authenticity, she openly shares her wisdom from hard-earned life lessons through stories resonating with anyone navigating loneliness, grief, healing, reinvention, or change.

Lisa's writing and talks invite others to embrace vulnerability, reclaim their voice, and live with intentional positivity. She is the author of *Oh Hello, Alzheimer's*, a moving account of her journey as a caregiver to her late husband Peter, who was diagnosed with early-onset Alzheimer's. In her second book, *Find Joy, No Regrets*, Lisa explores what came after—grief, rediscovery, and the profound power of choice. Her reflections on love, loss, bullying, growth, and inner peace offer readers a roadmap for living fully, even when life doesn't go as planned.

Lisa is also a contributing author to *Chicken Soup for the Soul: Navigating Elder Care and Dementia*. She serves as the Executive Chair of the Greater Hartford Walk to End Alzheimer's and serves as an Alzheimer's Association Board Member. She frequently speaks at conferences and memory care communities, offering compassionate support, practical strategies, and guidance to both professionals and families

She lives in Connecticut with her fiancé Jonathan, where their life together is filled with laughter, deep conversation, and shared moments of joy. They are surrounded by their blended families and a close-knit circle of friends who enrich their days with connection, community and meaning. Whether advocating, writing, speaking, or simply showing up for others, Lisa's mission remains clear: to spread hope, celebrate resilience, live presently, and remind others of the joy that's always possible—even after heartbreak.

To connect with Lisa, learn more, or share your story, please visit her OhHelloAlz.com, @OhHelloAlzheimers, @FindJoyNoRegrets,

www.ingramcontent.com/pod-product-compliance
Lightning Source LLC
Chambersburg PA
CBHW060142130626
46556CB00006B/2458